Historical American Biographies

AMELIA EARHART

Legend of Flight

Lynda Pflueger

Enslow Publishers, Inc.

40 Industrial Road   PO Box 38
Box 398   Aldershot
Berkeley Heights, NJ 07922   Hants GU12 6BP
USA   UK

http://www.enslow.com

To my SCBWI chapter in San Diego, California.

Library of Congress Cataloging-in-Publication Data

Pflueger, Lynda.
 Amelia Earhart : legend of flight / Lynda Pflueger.
  p. cm. — (Historical American biographies)
 Summary: A biography of Amelia Earhart who, four years after becoming the first woman passenger to fly across the Atlantic Ocean, became the first woman pilot to do so, as well.
 Includes bibliographical references and index.
 ISBN 0-7660-1976-4
 1. Earhart, Amelia, 1897–1937—Juvenile literature. 2. Women air pilots—United States—Biography—Juvenile literature. 3. Air pilots—United States—Biography—Juvenile literature. [1. Earhart, Amelia, 1897-1937. 2. Air pilots. 3. Women—Biography.] I. Title. II. Series.
TL540.E3 P48 2004
629.13'092—dc21

                              2002152633

Printed in the United States of America

10 9 8 7 6 5 4 3 2 1

To Our Readers:
We have done our best to make sure all Internet Addresses in this book were active and appropriate when we went to press. However, the author and the publisher have no control over and assume no liability for the material available on those Internet sites or on other Web sites they may link to. Any comments or suggestions can be sent by e-mail to comments@enslow.com or to the address on the back cover.

Illustration Credits: Enslow Publishers, Inc., pp. 80, 106–107, 112; The National Air and Space Museum, Smithsonian Institution, pp. 4, 43, 76, 98; National Archives and Records Administration, pp. 7, 65; Reproduced from the Collections of the Library of Congress, pp. 84, 99; The Schlesinger Library, Radcliffe Institute, Harvard University, pp. 11, 13, 17, 23, 26, 37, 39, 53, 62, 71.

Cover Illustration: The National Air and Space Museum, Smithsonian Institution (Background and Earhart portrait).

CONTENTS

Amelia Earhart

Solo Across the Atlantic

Women must try to do things as men have tried.
When they fail their failure must be but a challenge
to others.[1]

—Amelia Earhart

In 1928, Amelia Earhart was the first woman to fly across the Atlantic Ocean as a passenger. Four years later, she was determined to make the flight again. This time she was going to pilot her own plane.

At dusk on May 20, 1932, Earhart took off from Harbour Grace, Newfoundland, in Canada, headed for Paris, France. She preferred to take off at night rather than during the day and risk landing "on an unknown shore" in the dark.[2] Her altimeter, the

instrument that displays how high a plane is flying, went crazy shortly after the flight began. The hands on the dial swung around and around aimlessly. "I knew the instrument was out of commission for the rest of the flight," Earhart wrote.[3]

Around 11:30 P.M., she ran into a severe storm with lightning. Her plane was knocked about by the storm for nearly an hour. She had trouble maintaining her course. When she reached calmer weather, she was flying blind in the clouds and decided to fly above them.

For about half an hour she slowly gained altitude. Then she realized ice was forming on the windshield and air speed indicator. She had no choice but to drop down to warmer air. As she descended, the plane went into a spin. "How long we spun I do not know . . . I do know that I tried my best to do exactly what one should do with a spinning airplane, and regained flying control as the warmth of the lower altitude melted the ice," Earhart wrote.[4]

When she came out of the spin, she could see the ocean's waves breaking beneath her. "As my altimeter was out of commission, I could not tell whether I was 50 feet off the water or 150. I only know I was too close. . . ." Earhart later wrote.[5] She was in a dangerous position and spent the rest of the night plowing through the clouds, trying to maintain a safe distance above the water.

Amelia Earhart is welcomed in Londonderry, Ireland, after her solo flight across the Atlantic Ocean.

At dawn, she could see the traces of ice that had gathered on the wings of her plane. "Probably, if I had been able to see what was happening on the outside during the night, I would have had heart failure then and there; but, as I could not see, I carried on."[6] When she switched to one of her reserve fuel tanks in the cockpit, she found that her gas gauge was not working properly and gasoline started dripping down the side of her neck.

Due to the trouble she encountered, Earhart thought it was best to land as soon as possible. She headed east for Ireland. She was greatly relieved when she spotted a small fishing vessel and then the rocky coastline of Ireland.

A little later, she came across railroad tracks and followed them, hoping they would lead her to a town with a landing field. Finding only a small village, she landed in a cow pasture and taxied to a nearby farmhouse. Several surprised people emerged from the house and greeted her. "Have you flown far?" one of the men asked.

"From America," she replied.[7]

Despite tremendous odds, Amelia Earhart was the first woman to fly solo across the Atlantic.

2

EARLY YEARS

I was named for my grandmother and was lent her for company during the winter months.[1]

—Amelia Earhart

Amelia Earhart was born in Atchison, Kansas, in the middle of a summer heat wave. She was the first child of Amelia Harres Otis and Edwin Stanton Earhart. Her mother, whom everyone called Amy, was also born in Atchison, in 1869. (The exact day and month are unknown.) Amy was the eldest daughter in a family of eight children.

Amelia's father, Edwin, was the youngest of twelve children. His father was a Lutheran minister. Edwin was born in Kansas on March 28, 1867. At the age of fourte, he received a scholarship to

attend Thiel College, a Lutheran school in Greenville, Pennsylvania. Four years later, at the age of eighteen, he was the youngest student to graduate in the history of the school. After teaching for a year, he went to The University of Kansas in Lawrence to study the law. He worked his way through school by shining shoes, tending furnaces, and tutoring his classmates.

Parents Meet

Edwin and Amy met during the summer of 1890 at a garden party. Amy was a debutante and the party was being held at the Otis home to formally introduce her to Atchison's society. Mark Otis, Amy's older brother, brought Edwin, his college roommate, home with him to attend the party. When introducing his sister to Edwin, Mark said, "This is Edwin Earhart, the law student who has pulled me through this year's examinations!"[2]

Amy immediately liked the tall, handsome, and charming young man. He was intelligent, loved books, and best of all was studying to be a lawyer like her father. Edwin was captivated by Amy and let her know he liked her, too. He began to court her.

Alfred Otis, Amy's father, was not pleased with the match. Otis, a self-made man and retired U.S. District Court judge, had high hopes for his favorite daughter. He wanted her to marry into a wealthy and socially prominent family. Edwin's parents were very poor and, as far as Otis was concerned, members of the wrong religion. Judge Otis was a leader in his church, the Trinity Episcopal Church.

Amy stubbornly persisted. Her father finally gave his consent. However, Edwin had to earn at least fifty dollars a month before they could marry.

In 1894, Edwin graduated from law school. Then he went to work as a lawyer settling claims on a fee-for-services basis for railroad companies. It took a year before he earned fifty dollars a month.

Parents' Wedding

Amy and Edwin were finally married, five years after they met, in a simple ceremony in the Trinity Episcopal Church. The ceremony was held on Wednesday, October 16, 1895, at 11:00 A.M. It was a small affair. Only some relatives of the couple and "their more intimate friends" were

This portrait of Earhart's parents, Amy Otis Earhart and Edwin Earhart, was taken on October 16, 1895.

invited.[3] But, Edwin's father, a Lutheran minister, probably did not attend. His wife, Mary, had recently died. In addition, he would have gone against his church's doctrine by approving of his son's marriage to an Episcopalian.[4]

No reception was held after the ceremony. Amy and Edwin went from the church to the train station. They caught the noon train bound for Kansas City, Kansas, where they would make their home. Alfred Otis had bought his daughter and new son-in-law a small white frame house at 1021 Ann Avenue as a wedding gift. The house was completely furnished and included a library of law books.[5]

For Amy Earhart, the transition from pampered daughter to housewife was a difficult one. She was not used to doing housework and budgeting her money. When she became pregnant, her parents insisted she come home where she could be cared for by her family.[6]

On July 24, 1897, at 11:30 P.M., Amelia Mary Earhart was born in Atchison, Kansas. She was named after her two grandmothers, Amelia Harres Otis and Mary Wells Earhart. Amy described her daughter as an "eight and a half pounder" who had "a beautifully shaped head and nice hands, a real water color baby with the bluest of blue eyes, rosy cheeks and red lips . . ."[7] Amy took Amelia home to Kansas City.

Lives With Her Grandparents

When Amelia was three years old, she "was lent" to her grandmother Amelia Otis "for company" in the winter months.[8] Her grandmother, who still lived in Atchison, was lonesome. Amelia Otis's mother, Maria Harres, who had lived with her for thirty years, died. Then her eldest son, William, and his wife died. Finally, her youngest daughter, Margaret, married and moved to Philadelphia, taking her first grandchild, William's daughter Annie, with her. Even Alfred Otis was dismayed by all the family members who had either died or moved away in such a short period.

Amy was relieved to have her mother caring for young Amelia. It was a good arrangement. Amy had just given birth to her second child, Grace Muriel Earhart, on December 29, 1899.

Amelia's living with her grandparents was not an unusual arrangement. Alfred Otis had also lived with his

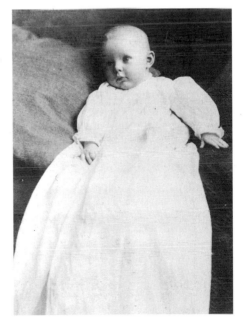

Earhart was four-and-a-half months old when this baby picture was taken.

Baby Book

Amy Earhart kept a baby book entitled *Queer Doings and Quaint Sayings of Baby Earhart* in which she wrote down the details of her baby girl's activities. In the book, she wrote that Amelia "sleeps all the time," and never sucks her thumb.[9] She documented when Amelia took her first steps, at the age of eleven months, and that by two years of age she often sang herself to sleep. The final entry in Amelia's baby book is the most revealing about her personality. Her mother wrote, "I overheard her talking to herself and on her discovering me in the room she said, 'If you are not here to talk to I just whisper in my own ears.'"[10]

grandparents for several years. Amelia's mother and sister came to visit often. The main drawback of the arrangement was that Amelia rarely saw her father. He rarely visited Atchison and Amelia was used to spending alot of time with him. In fact, her first word had been "Papa" instead of "Mama."

3

TOMBOY

I know that I worried my grandmother considerably by running home from school and jumping over the fence. . . .[1]

—Amelia Earhart

In her grandparents' home, Amelia was given a bedroom of her own. From the window in her bedroom, she could see the Missouri River. Along with her doting grandmother, there was Mary Brashay, the Irish cook, and Charlie Parks, the gardener, to look after her.

While living with her grandparents, Amelia grew to be tall for her age and so thin that her friends called her Skinny. Her eyes were blue-gray, and she had freckles. Her long blond hair was usually parted

in the middle. She liked to wear it in ponytails tied back with large ribbons, a style that was popular at the time. Shunning dolls, Amelia preferred her wooden toy donkey.

One of Amelia's favorite pastimes was jumping fences. The first time her grandmother caught her leaping over their fence, she told her, "Ladies don't climb fences, child. Only boys do that. Little girls use the gate."[2] Amelia, an independent soul, was not deterred. Instead, she would look before she leaped to make sure her grandmother was not watching.

Amelia never wanted for friends. Her sister Muriel, whom she called Pidge, came to visit often. Also, her Challis cousins lived next door. Lucy, who was nicknamed Toot, was two years younger than Amelia. Then came Kathryn, who was five years younger and went by the nickname Katch. The baby of the family was Peggy. Also, two blocks away lived Virginia Park, whose nickname was Ginger, and her sister Ann.

Amelia was bold, brave, and ready for any adventure. According to Ann Park she was always the leader. "She would dare anything; we would all follow along."[3] Of their childhood together Katch later said, "I just adored her. . . . She was not only fun . . . she could do *everything*."[4]

This family photograph was taken in 1904. From left to right in the back are Carl Otis, Amelia Otis, Anna Otis, Amy Earhart, and Edwin Earhart. In the front, are Muriel Earhart (left) and Amelia Earhart (right).

Bogie

One of Amelia and her playmates' favorite things to do was to play a pretend game called Bogie. They made the game up themselves and it involved going on imaginary journeys in an old abandoned carriage that was stored in the Otis barn. In one adventure, called "The Pursuit of the Hairy Men," Amelia and her friends were pioneers traveling to an imaginary place they called Pearyville. Pretending to be boys, the girls placed sawhorses in front of the carriage and equipped themselves with fake wooden pistols. Shortly after beginning their journey, they were attacked by a group of hairy men. They shouted, "Oh hairy men hairy men," and pointed their pistols and shouted "bangbang."[5] The hairy men would have carried the girls off forever if Amelia had not remembered that the hairy men were afraid of red and produced a red gumdrop to scare them away. They continued on their journey through all sorts of other dangers such as giant spiders, snakes, witches,

Close Call

At the time of Amelia's childhood, boys were permitted to ride their sleds downhill lying down, but girls were expected to assume a more ladylike posture and sit up. Amelia, of course, defied convention and often rode her sled lying down. One winter's day, she was sliding down a steep hill near the edge of town, when a junk man's cart suddenly appeared on the road beneath her. The horse pulling the cart was wearing enormous blinders blocking his vision. Amelia could not turn or stop and the junk man did not hear her screams. Within seconds, she slid between the front and back legs of the horse. It was a close call. If she had been sitting up, her head or the horse's ribs would have suffered from the collision.[6]

ghosts, and corpses. In the end they never reached Pearyville. That was part of the game, too.

Dad's Invention

Amelia spent her summers with her parents and sister in Kansas City. During those long, hot days, she played with her sister and they explored their neighborhood. Their constant companion was their big black dog, named James Ferocious. They liked to decorate him with ribbons and harness him to a small cart.

In the evenings, when Edwin Earhart came home from work, he often played cowboys and Indians with his daughters. After dinner, the girls' favorite pastime was watching him work on his invention: a device that would hold the required signal flags at the end of a train. Edwin Earhart told his family his invention would "bring our ship in."[7] He hoped to make a fortune for his family by patenting and selling his invention.

In May 1903, he traveled to Washington, D.C., to obtain a patent. He used the money that had been set aside to pay the property taxes on his home to pay for the trip. When he arrived in the Patent Office in Washington, D.C., he discovered that a man from Colorado had already obtained a patent on a device identical to his.

Several months later, the Kansas City tax collector visited the Earhart home to collect delinquent property taxes. Amy Earhart was sure her husband had paid the taxes until she found out he had used the money. She was embarrassed and fearful of losing her home. Quickly, Edwin Earhart tried to resolve the problem. He sold a valuable collection of law books that his father-in-law had given him. Unfortunately, one of the lawyers who bought the books bragged to Alfred Otis about his purchase. Amelia's grandfather was outraged. As far as he was concerned, this was another of his son-in-law's many irresponsible acts.

World's Fair

During the summer of 1904, Edwin Earhart made an extra one hundred dollars. Instead of saving the money, he took his family on a weeklong vacation to see the World's Fair in St. Louis, Missouri. Amelia, who was seven years old, rode an elephant and a Ferris wheel with her father while her mother and little sister watched. She was also fascinated by a roller coaster, but her mother would not let her ride it.

Roller Coaster

When Amelia returned home, she decided to build a roller coaster in her backyard. With the help of her friends and one of her uncles, Amelia constructed wooden tracks and nailed them to the roof of a tool shed in her backyard. They attached buggy wheels to an old cart and greased the wheels with lard, a type of fat, they found in the icebox.

Amelia insisted on being the first one to ride the cart down the tracks. She made a crash landing and decided they needed to add additional track so the cart would make a slower descent. Her second attempt down the track was successful, and she proclaimed it was "just like flying."[8] However, all the noise brought her mother outside to see what was going on. Amy Earhart felt the homemade roller coaster was terribly dangerous for little girls and insisted it be torn down. Amelia pleaded but her mother would not listen.

Muriel thought that if their father had been home, they would have been allowed to keep their roller coaster. She felt he "was in favor of them being as much like boys" as they wanted.[9]

4

MAVERICK

In fact, I think it is just about the most important thing any girl can do—try herself out, do something.[1]

—Amelia Earhart

In 1907, when Amelia was ten years old, her father was offered a position as a claims agent with the Rock Island Railroad. The job guaranteed a regular monthly salary and represented Edwin Earhart's first step on the ladder to success. Amelia's mother encouraged her husband to accept the position. A regular salary meant the end to her family's strict budgeting and penny-pinching. The only drawback was that they would have to move to Des Moines, Iowa.

At the age of ten, Amelia was still staying with her grandparents in Atchison, Kansas, while her parents looked for a house in Des Moines, Iowa.

Amelia and Muriel spent the summer with their grandparents in Atchison while their parents were house hunting in Des Moines. Due to the summer heat, the Earhart sisters often had to play inside the cool house. One of their favorite pastimes was reading in their grandparents' library. The library was filled with classics such as *Black Beauty* and *The Tale of Peter Rabbit*. There was also a large collection of magazines that had been bound into books. The bound volumes were too heavy to hold in the girls' laps, so they read the books while lying on the floor on their stomachs. The collection included *Harper's Young People*, *The Youth's Companion*, and *Harper's Weekly*. The magazines were filled with boys' adventure stories, which the girls eagerly read. According to Muriel, they skipped the "many pages of the moralizing" telling them what they should or should not do.[2] They preferred to go right to the action.

In the fall, since their parents had not found adequate housing in Des Moines, the girls attended a small private school, the College Preparatory School, in Atchison. Amelia liked school and her grades reflected it. She earned either E's, for *excellent*, or VG's, for *very good*, in all her subjects. Her classes included reading, spelling, writing, math, English, French, geography, and sewing.

Des Moines, Iowa

During the summer of 1908, the girls finally joined their parents in Des Moines. In July, to celebrate Amelia's eleventh birthday, the family attended the Iowa State Fair. At the fair, Amelia saw her first airplane. She later remarked, "It was a thing of rusty wire and wood and not at all interesting."[3] She admitted that she was more intrigued by a paper hat shaped like a peach basket that she had just purchased for fifteen cents.[4]

In the fall, the girls were enrolled in their local public school. When school officials suggested that Amy Earhart cut her daughters' hair to prevent them from catching head lice, she hired a teacher to tutor the girls at home. Their new teacher added poetry and music to their regular lessons.

The following year, Edwin Earhart was promoted again. His salary doubled and he became the head of a department of five claims adjusters. His name was prominently listed on the company's letterhead, and he had his own secretary and the use of a private railroad car for both business and pleasure. With her husband's success, Amy was able to hire a cook and a maid. In addition, the family moved to a more fashionable part of town. It was a happy time for the Earhart family.

Summer Vacations

To escape the hot summers in Des Moines, Amy Earhart and her daughters spent several summers in Worthington, on Lake Okabena in southwestern Minnesota. In Worthington, a small farming community, they rented rooms on a farm owned by Clinton Mann. They ate their meals at a nearby boarding house. Amelia and Muriel made friends with the Manns' daughters and enjoyed helping with chores around the farm. They also liked to ride the Manns' pony, Prince.

Amelia later wrote that Prince "could be bribed by cookies to do almost anything."[5] The cookies were one of Amelia's creations, and she called them horse pies. They consisted of a bottom layer of tender

From left to right, Amelia Earhart, Muriel Earhart, their father Edwin Earhart, and his porter Tomko stand at the end of a railroad car.

Dr. Bones

In a pasture near the Mann farm, twelve-year-old Amelia discovered a pile of bones from three cows that had died during a winter blizzard. Fascinated, Amelia spent hours trying to sort out the bones to form a complete skeleton. She spent so much time on the project that the people of Worthington began to call her Dr. Bones.[6]

grass, a layer of sugar cookies, and then clover topped with Prince's name spelled out in mulberries.[7]

Dad's Sickness

Unfortunately, Edwin Earhart turned to alcohol. His drinking began slowly, with an occasional drink after work with his colleagues. Then it became common for him to drink every night after work and come home drunk and in a bad mood. Trying to hide their father's condition, the Earhart sisters called it "Dad's sickness."[8] In time, he began drinking at lunchtime and then would go back to work drunk. His loyal staff tried to cover for him, but he began making huge errors. Finally, Edwin's boss found him drunk at his desk and fired him. Afterward, Edwin spent a month in a sanatorium where he rested and tried to quit drinking. When he returned, Amelia and Muriel thought they had their "old dad back again," but it did not last.[9] It was the beginning of the breakup of their family.

In 1911, when Amelia was fourteen years old and Muriel eleven, Edwin Earhart left his wife. Amy wrote pleading letters to her husband begging him to return. As she always had, she forgave him no matter what he did. Finally, he returned but continued to drink heavily.

At this point Amy Earhart had no choice but to confide in her parents. They were appalled and did everything they could to try to talk her into getting a divorce. They even offered to take care of her and their granddaughters. Divorce, as far as Amy was concerned, was out of the question.

The following year, Amelia Otis died. In her will, she left half of her estate to her husband and the other half to her four living children. To prevent her son-in-law from drinking away her daughter's inheritance, she stipulated that Amy's inheritance would be held in trust for twenty years, or until Edwin's death. Her brother Mark Otis was named as the trustee. To add insult to injury, the Atchison newspaper, *The Atchison Globe*, printed the terms of Amelia Otis's will on the front page of the paper on February 14, 1912.

Three months later, on May 7, 1912, Alfred Otis died. The stipulations that had been in his wife's will were identical in his will. Amy's inheritance would go into a trust to be administered by her brother. Once again, *The Atchison Globe* printed the terms of the will. It was another blow for Edwin Earhart. He used to try to hide his drinking problem, but now he did not care who knew about it.

St. Paul, Minnesota

In 1913, after many months of being able to find only piecemeal work, Edwin Earhart was offered a clerk's position with the Great Northern Railroad in St. Paul, Minnesota. In hopes that things would be better in St. Paul, the Earharts moved. They rented a large house at 825 Fairmont Avenue, which proved to be a disaster. The house was so large, they could not afford to pay for the coal that was required to heat it and ended up closing off a majority of the rooms. Amelia and Muriel helped their mother save money by shopping for food miles away from their house, where prices were lower, and sometimes walking instead of paying bus fare.

Several months after they moved to St. Paul, Edwin Earhart returned home one evening and told his family to get his traveling bag out of the closet. There had been a freight-train wreck and his boss wanted him to look over the damage. He was to be in charge of representing the railroad when claims were presented. While Amy Earhart was fixing dinner, Amelia and Muriel helped their father pack.

During dinner, Amelia was unusually quiet. While clearing the table, Muriel asked her why.

Amelia opened a kitchen cabinet and showed her a bottle of whiskey she had found in her father's travel bag. They decided to get rid of it. Quickly, Amelia broke the seal, pried the cork out of the bottle, and began to pour it down the kitchen drain. Edwin Earhart appeared at the kitchen doorway and realized what his daughter was doing. He leaped across the kitchen and yelled at her to stop. Amy Earhart heard her husband's raised voice and ran into the kitchen just in time to stop him from striking Amelia. When he calmed down, Edwin apologized. He told Amelia that he wanted the whiskey to help keep him warm on the cold nights while he was away. He admitted, though, that now that it was gone, he would be better off without it.

Easter Outfits

The Earharts were living on Edwin's small salary, which covered only their rent, and the interest Amy earned from her trust fund. When spring came, there was no extra money for new Easter outfits for church. While rummaging around in their attic, Amelia found a solution to their problem. From custom-made silk drapes her mother had never used, she fashioned new Easter outfits. Muriel was put in charge of dying the cloth. She chose green for her outfit, and Amelia chose brown. Then Amelia made a pattern and sewed the outfits together. As they were leaving the house on Easter morning for church, Amelia yelled out the window at Muriel, "If it should rain, for heaven's sakes, take off your hat and get under shelter before you leave a trail of green dye on the sidewalk."[10]

Springfield, Missouri

After a year of living in St. Paul, Edwin Earhart came home and announced they were moving to Springfield, Missouri. He had been offered a job there with the railroad. After a tedious seven-hour journey in a hot, crowded passenger car, they arrived in Springfield only to find that the man Edwin Earhart was to replace had decided not to retire. The railroad agreed to pay them back for their traveling expenses but could offer Edwin only part-time work for a month.

For Amy Earhart that was the last straw. The stress of the last few years had caught up with her. She was exhausted and knew her daughters needed a break. Choosing her words carefully, she reminded her husband that their friends in Chicago, the Shedd family, had invited them to come and live with them until he could find work. She felt it was time they accepted their offer.

Edward Earhart argued with his wife. Finally, it was agreed that Amy, Amelia, and Muriel would go to Chicago and he would stay in Springfield for a

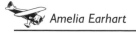

month. Then he would return to St. Paul where he would try to establish his own law office. A letter was quickly sent to the Shedds, who promptly replied in a telegram, "Our home is your home now until next year or longer."[11]

When they arrived in Chicago, Amy Earhart enrolled her daughters in high school. Muriel entered Morgan Park High School where one of the Shedd daughters attended. Amy let seventeen-year-old Amelia choose what high school she wanted to attend. Amelia refused to go to Morgan Park because she said their chemistry laboratory consisted of only a kitchen sink. After visiting several high schools within commuting distance, she chose Hyde Park High School.

During the school year, Amelia tried to have an incompetent English teacher fired by circulating a petition. The teacher, who was hard of hearing, just sat at her desk in the classroom and let her students do whatever they wanted. When her classmates refused to sign her petition, Amelia took the matter into her own hands. She convinced the school librarian that she had an assignment that would require her to spend every English period in the library. She never returned to the teacher's class.

5

FIRST FLIGHT

As soon as we left the ground, I knew I myself had to fly.[1]

—Amelia Earhart

While separated from his family, Edwin Earhart moved to Kansas City, Missouri. He stayed with his elderly sister, Mary Woodworth, and continued to revive his law practice. He sobered up and started straightening out his life. In time, he managed to persuade his wife and daughters to join him. They were reunited in the fall of 1915.

Shortly after the family was reunited, Edwin Earhart convinced his wife to file a lawsuit against her brother and attempt to break the terms of her parents' will. Amy Earhart hated the thought of

dragging her family's problems into a courtroom. Her husband's pleas and the dwindling interest payments from her trust fund forced her to take action.

Dr. Charles Johnson, Amelia Otis's physician, testified in court that his patient "was unduly harassed by worry and illness."[2] He said that she did not realize she had placed her eldest daughter "in the same category as Theodore Otis, her son, who had been all his life mentally retarded . . . ."[3] On February 17, 1917, the Atchison County District Court ordered Mark Otis to turn over all of Amy Earhart's inheritance except for the funds held by the Northern Trust Company. Two months later, Mark Otis suddenly died and she gained control of all her inheritance.

Now that she had the funds, Amy Earhart decided to send her daughters to private schools to prepare them for college. Muriel wanted to be a teacher. She decided to enroll in St. Margaret's in Toronto, Canada. Amelia chose the elite Ogontz School in Philadelphia, Pennsylvania.

Ogontz School

At Ogontz, Earhart plunged into school activities. In a letter to her mother, she described her daily schedule. At 7:00 A.M. every day, she was awakened by the sound of a cowbell. Then she spent an hour saying her prayers and getting dressed for school.

Breakfast was served at 8:00 A.M., followed by a morning walk. Her classes began at 9:00 A.M. and ended at 1:15 P.M. In the afternoon, she played hockey, tennis, or participated in a mandatory military drill. During the drill, the girls wore uniforms and marched carrying wooden guns. The activity was popular with many of the girls. Earhart, however, thought that drill was "awful."[4] From 4:00 to 5:00 P.M., she attended study hall. Dinner was served at 6:00 P.M., and every evening except Saturday and Monday there was an after-dinner activity. Earhart ended her letter with the comment that "every minute" of her day was accounted for and "you have to go by schedule."[5]

Earhart excelled in her studies at Ogontz. Her grades were either G, for *good*, or G+, for *excellent*, in all her subjects except Bible study. She also found time to devour books that were not part of the school curriculum. So much so, that the school's headmistress, Abby Sutherland, commented, "Earhart was always pushing into unknown seas in her reading."[6]

Money was still tight for the Earharts. Compared to the other girls at Ogontz, Earhart was poor. She never complained, and in her letters tried to reassure her mother that she could make do with the clothes she had. Abby Sutherland thought Earhart handled the situation with great poise, for "her style

of dressing was always simple and becoming" and she helped impress upon "the overindulged girls . . . the beauty and comfort of simple dressing."[7]

World War I

During Christmas vacation of her second year at Ogontz, Earhart went to Toronto, Canada, to be with her sister for the holidays. The previous year the United States had entered the war in Europe, but it was not until Earhart went to Toronto that she realized the tragedy of war. She later wrote, "Instead of new uniforms and brass bands, I saw only the results of a four years' desperate struggle; men without arms and legs, men who were paralyzed and men who were blind."[8]

Earhart could not bear the thought of going back to school. She stayed in Canada and enrolled in a first-aid course given by the Voluntary Aid Detachment of the St. John Ambulance Brigade. After graduating, she went to work as a nurse's aide in the children's wing of Victoria Memorial Hospital and then transferred to Spadina Military Hospital.

Earhart later wrote that she "hotfooted here and there to attend" to her patients' needs.[9] She worked six days a week from seven in the morning until seven at night, with a two-hour break every afternoon. Due to her knowledge of chemistry, she spent

Amelia Earhart is dressed in her nursing uniform in Toronto, Canada, during World War I.

most of her time in the kitchen and later in the pharmacy.

During the winter of 1918, Earhart often spent her days off visiting her former patients who were pilots at the local airfield. This, she said, was when "I felt a first urge to fly."[10] At the time, no civilian was allowed to go up in a military plane. She "hung around in spare time and absorbed all I could."[11]

While attending the Toronto Fair with a girlfriend, she watched an exhibition of stunt flying. Before the exhibition was over, one of the pilots became bored and decided to fly low to the ground and watch the people run as he swooped over their heads. Earhart stood her ground but her friend ran. Later she wrote:

> Commonsense told me if something went wrong with the mechanism, or if the pilot lost control, he, the airplane, and I would be rolled up in a ball together. I did not understand it at the time but I believe that little red airplane said something to me as it swished by.[12]

Medicine

After the war ended, Earhart became a patient herself. Due to a severe sinus infection, she underwent minor surgery to drain her sinus passages. She spent several months recovering. During her recovery, she stayed with her sister, who was attending Smith College in Northampton, Massachusetts.

In the fall of 1919, at the age of twenty-two, Earhart enrolled in Columbia University in New York as a premed student. She signed up for the maximum units a student was allowed to carry and took numerous science courses. For fun, she sat in on a French poetry class. By the end of her second semester, she realized that she was not cut out to be a doctor. She liked the scientific aspects of medical research, but the practical side of dealing with patients did not appeal to her.

While Earhart and her sister were attending college, their parents moved to California. Once they were settled, they wanted their daughters to join them. Muriel needed to stay in Massachusetts until she graduated. Since Earhart had dropped out of college, she felt obligated to join her parents. She was somewhat bitter about going, for she knew her parents were still having problems with their marriage. As they parted, she remarked to her sister, "I'll see what I can do to keep Mother and Dad

together, Pidge, but after that I'm going to come back here and live my own life."[13]

"Aviation Caught Me"

After she arrived in California, Earhart's interest in flying led her to go to local air shows. After attending an air show at Daugherty Field in Long Beach with her father, she went on her first airplane ride the next day. "As soon as we left the ground, I knew I myself had to fly," Earhart later wrote.[14]

That evening Earhart told her parents that she wanted to learn how to fly. Since they could not afford to pay for her lessons, she went to work for the telephone company as a file clerk. From then on, she spent every weekend at Kinner Field in south Los Angeles. Her trip to the airport, by electric streetcar, took an hour. Then she walked several miles along a dusty road.

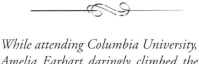

While attending Columbia University, Amelia Earhart daringly climbed the great dome on the top of the university library and had her picture taken by a friend with a Brownie camera.

Earhart chose a woman pilot, twenty-four-year-old Neta Snook, to be her first instructor. She felt she would be less self-conscious taking lessons from a woman than a man, and therefore she would learn more quickly. In her book, *I Taught Amelia to Fly*, Snook wrote about the first time she met Amelia Earhart. Snook was about to climb into her airplane when a tall, slender young woman approached her accompanied by an older man. Snook wrote:

> She was wearing a brown suit, plain but of a good cut. Her hair was braided and neatly coiled around her head; there was a light scarf around her neck and she carried gloves. She would have stood out in any crowd . . . The gentleman with her was slightly gray at the temples and wore a blue . . . business suit . . .

The young woman introduced herself: "I'm Amelia Earhart and this is my father . . ." Then she told Snook she wanted to learn how to fly and asked if she would teach her.[15]

Snook agreed to take daily payments for the lessons, as Earhart earned the money. Earhart's first flying lesson was on January 3, 1921. She arrived at the airfield wearing brown jodhpurs (breeches for horseback riding), boots laced to her midcalf, and a jacket. A book on aerodynamics was tucked under her arm. Aerodynamics is the scientific study of how objects move through the air.

Snook's Canuck had two open cockpits. A duplicate set of controls was in each cockpit, consisting of

Neta Snook

In her sophomore year of college, Neta Snook quit school and enrolled in a flying school. When the school abruptly closed, she walked, hitchhiked, and rode freight trains across the country to Newport News, Virginia, where she talked her way into an all-male flight instruction program at Curtiss School of Aviation. When World War I began, the school closed. After the war, Snook purchased a wrecked airplane, a Canuck, and took it to her home in Ames, Iowa, where she rebuilt it in her backyard. In order to fly year-round, Snook moved to California from Iowa.

a rudder bar and a stick. The rudder bar turned the plane right or left, depending on which way it was manipulated by the pilot's feet. The stick, which rose from the floor of the plane, made the plane dive downward when pushed forward and climb upward when pulled back. Snook occupied the cockpit in the rear of the plane and whenever she maneuvered the controls, the movements were duplicated in the forward cockpit where Earhart sat.

After receiving nineteen hours of instruction from Snook, Earhart decided she needed more "strenuous" instruction before she made her first solo flight.[16] She chose John "Monte" Montijo, a former pilot who had served in World War I. Later she wrote, "I refused to fly alone until I knew some

stunting. It seemed foolhardy to try to go up alone without the ability to recognize and recover quickly from any position the plane might assume, a reaction only possible with practice."[17]

Sam Chapman

While living in Los Angeles, Earhart began dating Sam Chapman, one of her parents' boarders. Chapman was tall, tanned, and good-looking. He had grown up in Massachusetts and had a degree in engineering. Earhart and Chapman had a lot in common. They enjoyed tennis, swimming, books, and the theater. In 1923, they became engaged.

First Airplane

On July 24, 1921, for Amelia's twenty-fourth birthday, her mother helped her purchase her first airplane, a used Kinner Airster. Now that she owned her own plane, Earhart felt she needed to dress the part and purchased a leather coat, helmet, and goggles. Her family was amused when she wore her new shiny leather coat around the house for several days to break it in and even slept in it one night "to give it some authentic wrinkles, too."[18]

For Earhart, learning to fly was a long, drawn-out process. Money was the problem. As she put it, "no pay, no fly and no work, no pay."[19] Finally, she made her first solo flight and took her plane up to an

Amelia Earhart poses while wearing her leather jacket and helmet and holding her goggles.

altitude of five thousand feet, played around for a little while, and then came back down. Other pilots asked her how she felt and if she did anything special. One pilot told her he had been so happy when he made his first solo flight that he sang as loud as he could. Later Earhart admitted that she had "felt silly" because she "hadn't done anything special" other than making "an exceptionally poor landing."[20]

Sets Record

In October, Earhart invited her father and sister to attend an air meet with her at Rogers Airfield in Los Angeles. In order to sell the public on flying, air meets were quite common. When they arrived at the field, Earhart handed her family their tickets and told them she could not sit with them.

A little later, the announcer told the crowd that a pilot was going to attempt to set a new altitude record. To their surprise, they watched Earhart

climb into her airplane, wave, and take off. They anxiously watched for her return. Nearly an hour later she landed and climbed out of her plane. She was immediately surrounded by officials. In a few minutes, the announcer shouted through his megaphone that Amelia Earhart had just set a new record for a woman by ascending to the height of fourteen thousand feet.

Shortly afterward, an article appeared in *The New York Times* newspaper regarding Earhart's feat. The article was also accompanied by a photograph of Earhart in her flying outfit. The publicity displeased several of her older family members. One uncle wrote to Earhart's mother and complained. He said that, "The only time a lady's name should appear in print is at her birth, her marriage, and her funeral."[21]

On May 16, 1923, Earhart was awarded a flying certificate, number 6017, from the Fédération Aéronautique Internationale (FAI). The certificate declared that the holder had completed all the requirements of the organization to be considered an "Aviator Pilot."[22] At the time, it was not necessary to have a pilot's license in order to fly a plane. As Earhart often explained, "People just flew, when and if they could, in anything which would get off the ground."[23] In order to set new FAI records, however, Earhart had to be a member of the organization.

Mine Investment

By the beginning of 1924, Amy Earhart's inheritance was almost gone. After sending her daughters to college and helping Earhart buy her first airplane, she had only twenty thousand dollars left. At the rate they were going, if the remaining funds were not invested in an endeavor that would give them a high return, there would soon be nothing left.

Earhart suggested that her mother invest in a small mine owned by one of her friends, Peter Barnes. Sam Chapman approved of the idea, and the Earharts decided it would be a sound investment. Unfortunately, shortly after they invested in the mine, it was destroyed by a flash flood. Then the mining company's only truck was hit by a train at a railroad crossing. Earhart felt extremely guilty about her mother's losing her inheritance. She sold her airplane in order to help her family with their financial problems. To add to her misery, her sinus problems returned; and, in the spring of 1924, her parents' marriage finally broke down for good. Edwin Earhart filed for a divorce.

6

SOCIAL WORK AND AVIATION

It usually works out that if one follows where an interest leads, the knowledge or contacts somehow or other will be found useful sometime.[1]

—Amelia Earhart

For over a year, Amelia Earhart had dreamed of flying back east to continue her education. She had already plotted her route, and her mother had agreed to go with her. However, the recurring pain in her head whenever she flew made the flight impossible. Instead of buying another airplane, she purchased a touring car called a Kissel and made plans to drive back east. The car had a convertible top, wire wheels, big nickel headlamps, spare tires mounted on the passenger doors, and black fenders.

Since the car was painted yellow, she nicknamed it The Yellow Peril.

In mid-June, she picked up her mother and headed north instead of east. Her mother asked where they were going. Earhart replied that she was going to surprise her. They drove into northern California and toured Sequoia and Yosemite National Parks. From there, they went to Crater Lake in southwest Oregon. Then they visited the towns of Banff and Lake Louise in Canada before heading south into northwest Wyoming to visit Yellowstone National Park. In Cheyenne, Wyoming, Amelia followed the Lincoln Highway heading east. Their final destination was Boston, Massachusetts, where Muriel had settled.

By the time they reached Boston, they had traveled more than seven thousand miles, and Earhart's car was covered with tourist stickers. Traveling cross-country in an automobile was unusual at the time. Wherever they stopped, people gathered around them to ask questions about their trip. Earhart later wrote, "the fact that my roadster was a cheerful canary color may have caused some of the excitement."[2]

Boston

After arriving in Boston, Earhart's sinus problems returned. Once again, surgery was necessary. This

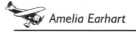

time her physician removed a small piece of bone in her nasal passage, which allowed her sinuses to finally drain. After a week's stay in the hospital, she was free from headaches and nasal discomfort for the first time in many years.

When she recovered from her surgery, Earhart began teaching English to foreign students enrolled in the Harvard University summer extension program. The classes were scheduled in the late afternoon and spread out in locations within a thirty-mile radius of Boston. Her wages and transportation allowance barely covered her expenses.

In the fall of 1925, Earhart answered a help-wanted ad in the newspaper for a novice social worker at the Denison House, one of Boston's oldest settlement houses. Immigrants often lived in settlement houses until they adjusted to their new home. Miss Marion Perkins, the principal, was impressed with Earhart when she applied for the job. She found her to be a "strikingly interesting girl" with an unusual vocabulary who "wants to write." She wrote on top of her application form "holds a sky pilots license!"[3] Despite Earhart's lack of social work experience, Miss Perkins hired her.

At the Denison House, Earhart worked mostly with Syrian and Chinese immigrants. As a part-time social worker, she was put in charge of the evening classes offered at the settlement house. Her

responsibilities also included teaching English and citizenship classes, explaining American customs to her clients, and organizing outings and games for their children. Occasionally, when a child needed specialized medical care, she would take him or her to the hospital in her car.

The children loved Earhart's car. Frequently, as many as ten children would stand on the running boards (steps attached below the car's door) while she drove slowly around the block. Often, they would beg her to drive past their homes, so they could show off and wave to their families.

Earhart was especially good with the children. Within a year, she was promoted and working full time at the Denison House running the kindergarten and programs for girls ages five to fourteen. She also moved into the Denison House. Her room was on the second floor and she ate her meals in the dining room with other resident workers. Occasionally, as a special treat, she would take several teenage girls home to her sister's house for a picnic or story-telling.

Broken Engagement

Sam Chapman followed Earhart to Massachusetts. He began working for the Edison Electric Company as an industrial heating engineer. He thought they would be getting married soon. Earhart, however,

was having second thoughts about marriage. She was not spending as much time with Chapman as he would have liked. He thought it was because he worked the night shift, so he tried to change his hours. This miffed Earhart and she told her sister, "He should do whatever makes him happiest. . . . I know what I want to do and I expect to do it married or single . . ."[4] Within a year, Earhart broke off their engagement but remained friends with Chapman.

Flying Again

Now that Earhart was working full time and earning thirty-five dollars a week, she took up her hobby of flying again. She joined the Boston chapter of the National Aeronautic Association and spent her free hours on weekends at the local airfields. Her name started appearing in local newspapers again. On May 26, 1927, she flew over Boston dropping free passes advertising a fund-raising event that would benefit the Denison House.[5] The Boston *Globe* newspaper interviewed her. She took full advantage of the opportunity to promote women and flying.

After seeing a photo of Ruth Nichols, another local pilot, in the *Boston Herald*, Earhart wrote her a letter asking her: What did she think of the idea "of forming an organization composed of women who fly?"[6] Earhart had been considering forming such an organization for some time. The two women exchanged many letters concerning the idea.

In 1928, Earhart was considering another clever idea to promote women and flying. She wanted to write an article for *The Bostonian*, a fashionable, well-read Boston magazine. She approached the magazine's editor, Katherine Crosby, with her idea. Crosby was charmed by Earhart and said that she was the most modest girl she had met in a long time. All Earhart wanted was to make flying interesting to women. Crosby had to persuade her to sign her article so that she would be given credit for writing it.

The article, entitled *When Women Go Aloft*, appeared in the May issue of the magazine, accompanied by a photograph of Earhart in her flying outfit. In her article, Earhart described the thrill of flying and some common misconceptions regarding the dangers of flying. She ended the article with a brief statement of her belief that, "There is no door closed to ability, so when women are ready there will be opportunity for them in aviation."[7]

Telephone Call

In April 1928, Amelia Earhart's life was changed forever. She was organizing a group of children for an activity when a young messenger told her she had a phone call. She told the messenger she was too busy to take the call. The caller persisted and finally

Earhart picked up the phone. The caller's name was Captain Hilton H. Railey. He introduced himself and then asked if she might be interested in doing something for aviation that might be considered hazardous.

Earhart was curious and asked for more details: Who was he, why had she been picked, and what were the specific details of the endeavor? Railey would not supply many details over the phone. He did furnish her with excellent references and made an appointment for her to meet with him in his office later that day. Earhart took Marion Perkins, her boss from the Denison House, with her for the interview.

When Hilton H. Railey first saw Earhart, he was convinced she was the right woman for the job. Not only was she a pilot, but she was also intelligent and had a great deal of poise. He found her resemblance to Colonel Charles Lindbergh, the first man to fly solo across the Atlantic, extraordinary. Within a short time he asked, "How would you like to be the first woman to fly the Atlantic?"[8]

Earhart pressed him for details. Railey told her that a wealthy American woman, Amy Phipps Guest, was sponsoring the flight. She had leased a Fokker F7 airplane from Commander Richard Byrd, the Arctic explorer, and named the plane *Friendship*. Guest had originally planned to accompany the crew and be the first woman to fly across the Atlantic. Due to her family's objections, she had abandoned the idea, but she still wanted "an American girl who would measure up to adequate standards of American womanhood" to make the flight.[9] Guest had recruited Railey and George Palmer Putnam, a New York publisher, to find an appropriate candidate.

Realizing she was being offered the opportunity of a lifetime, Earhart told Railey that she was interested in making the flight. She wanted to be more than just a passenger, though. She hoped to fly the plane for at least a short time if weather permitted. Railey gave her little encouragement because she

The plane Friendship *was able to take off from and land in water.*

did not know how to fly by instruments alone and had never flown a plane with three engines.

He also made it clear that the pilot and mechanic were being paid. He asked if she was prepared to receive no salary for being on the flight. She replied that she felt that the "privilege of being included in the expedition would be sufficient in itself."[10]

Railey asked her to keep the flight secret and told her he would be contacting her soon. Two weeks later, Earhart was asked to meet with Amy Guest's lawyer, David Layman, and her brother, John Phipps, in New York City. George Palmer Putnam would also be at the meeting. Putnam had another reason for being there. He published exploration and adventure books and thought he might have "stumbled on an adventure-in-the-making."[11] He had published Charles Lindbergh's book about his flight across the Atlantic. The book was a tremendous success. If Earhart was as great as his friend Hilton H. Railey said she was, he knew he had another potential best-seller on his hands.

During the meeting, Earhart knew that the men were sizing her up. She found it to be an embarrassing dilemma and later wrote, "If I were found wanting in too many ways I would be counted out. On the other hand, if I were just too fascinating, the gallant gentlemen might be loath [unwilling] to risk drowning me."[12]

Earhart worried unnecessarily. Two days after her meeting in New York, she received a note from Amy Guest and the formal agreement that had been drawn up by Guest's lawyer. She had the job if she wanted it. The contract stipulated that Earhart would be in charge while the plane was airborne, and her decisions would be final. In addition, Guest would pay all of Earhart's flight expenses.

Preparations for the Flight

The flight was shrouded in secrecy. Earhart did not dare go to the Boston Airport, where the plane was being prepared for the flight. She was too well known. When newspaper reporters came snooping around, they were told that the Fokker belonged to Commander Richard Byrd and he planned to use it in his second South Pole expedition.

No one knew Earhart was involved except Marion Perkins and her ex-fiancé Sam Chapman. Earhart did not even tell her family. When preparing for the flight she wrote what she called "popping off" letters to be opened only after her death. She entrusted the letters to George Putnam. To her father she wrote:

> Hooray for the grand adventure! I wish I had won, but it was worth while anyway. You know that. I have no faith we'll meet anywhere else, but I wish we might. Anyway, goodbye and good luck to you.[13]

To her mother she omitted her doubts about being reunited with her family in heaven and wrote:

> Even though I have lost, the adventure was worth while. Our family tends to be too secure. My life has really been very happy, and I didn't mind contemplating its end in the midst of it.[14]

The *Friendship* was equipped with three Wright Whirlwind 225 horsepower engines. The ship had a wingspan of seventy-two feet, and the wings were painted gold. The fuselage, or body of the ship, was orange. The bright colors were not chosen for artistic reasons. The orange paint, technically called chrome yellow, could be seen farther away than any other color. In the cabin space normally occupied by passengers, two large gas tanks were installed. In order to make the trip across the Atlantic, the crew planned to carry nine hundred gallons of fuel. The plane was fitted with pontoons so it could land in water. The pontoons were a safety feature. However, they also made it more difficult for the plane to take off with a heavy load. Fully loaded the plane weighed more than five tons.

The crew consisted of a pilot, Bill Stultz, and a mechanic, Louis "Slim" Gordon. Twenty-eight-year-old Stultz was from Williamsburg, Pennsylvania. He had spent two years in the Army Air Service followed by three years in the Naval Air Service. Afterward he worked extensively in commercial aviation. Slim

Gordon was from San Antonio, Texas, and a year younger than Stultz. He was also a veteran of the Army Air Service. For over a year he had been a flight mechanic for Reynolds Airways. Commander Byrd, who was acting as technical advisor to the flight, had recommended Stultz. Gordon was Stultz's choice as the mechanic. Earhart was pleased with the crew. She considered them "the best in the way of flying ability."[15]

Friendship **Flight**

By the end of May, the plane was ready. Twice they tried to take off from Boston's harbor. The first time there was too much wind, and the second, too much fog. Finally, on June 3, 1928, after lightening their load, they were off, headed for the coast of Trepassey, Newfoundland, in Canada. At Trepassey, they planned to fill their fuel tanks. Due to weather conditions, they were only able to make it to Halifax, Nova Scotia, also in Canada. The following day, around nine in the morning, they took off, headed for Trepassey.

In Trepassey, the weather gave them a great deal of trouble. They spent thirteen days waiting for weather conditions to improve so they could take off again. Several times they attempted to leave, but were unsuccessful due to either too much fog or too little wind. Boredom became a problem and Bill

Stultz began drinking. At one point Earhart thought about canceling the flight. Finally, they were able to take off on June 17.

In her logbook Earhart wrote that "our Atlantic crossing was literally a voyage in the clouds." They rarely saw the water beneath them.[16] At one point, Earhart likened the clouds to "fantastic gobs of mashed potatoes."[17] They also ran into a wind-and-rain storm that Earhart claimed was the "heaviest storm" she had "ever been in, in the air, and had to go through."[18]

After nearly eighteen hours in the air, their radio stopped working and they had no idea where they were. Suddenly, the fog thinned and they could see a patch of water beneath them. Almost miraculously

Traveled Light

On her first flight across the Atlantic, Earhart wore her old flying clothes: brown broadcloth breeches (pants designed for horseback riding), high laced boots, her ancient leather jacket, a light leather flying helmet, and goggles. To spruce up her outfit she added a silk blouse with a red necktie, a homely brown sweater, and a brown-and-white silk scarf around her neck. To keep warm on the flight she borrowed a heavy fur-lined flying suit that covered her from head to toe, including her shoes, from a friend. In a small army knapsack, she carried a toothbrush, comb, a few fresh handkerchiefs, and a tube of cold cream.

a big ship appeared. They circled the vessel, hoping the captain would have his crew paint the bearings of their location on his deck. When nothing happened, they wrote out a note to the captain and put it in a bag with a couple of oranges. Earhart tried to drop it through the hatchway on the plane onto the deck of the boat. Her dive-bombing was unsuccessful. The bag fell into the sea unnoticed.

With less than two hours of gas left, they continued to head eastward. In a short time, they spotted two more boats. They had no way of knowing it, but they had passed Ireland and were now headed for Wales. It was a great relief when they sighted land. They followed the shore until they located a safe harbor and landed the plane in the water at Burry Port, Wales, twenty hours and forty minutes after they left Trepassey.

Stultz tied the *Friendship* to a heavy buoy about a half mile from shore and they waited for someone to come out and welcome them. Evidently, a seaplane landing in the harbor was not unusual. Three men, who had been working at the water's edge, looked over at the plane and then went back to work. Gordon crawled out on one of the pontoons and yelled for someone to send out a boat. No one responded. Earhart decided to take the matter into her own hands. She waved a white towel, the signal

of distress, out an open window. A gentleman on the shore took off his coat and waved back at her.

Finally, boats came out to greet them. It took several hours, however, before the *Friendship* was safely tied up to the dock and the crew was able to disembark. They were welcomed by ten thousand enthusiastic Welshmen with only three policemen to help them get through the crowd.

7

CELEBRITY

The next time I fly anywhere, I shall do it alone![1]
—Amelia Earhart

After the *Friendship* flight, Amelia Earhart had planned to return to the work she loved, social work at the Denison House.[2] In Burry Port, she began to realize that she might never be able to go back to her old life. She found the media blitz that surrounded her amazing. As soon as the crew of the *Friendship* flight checked into the local hotel, they were barraged by reporters who were more interested in Earhart than Stultz or Gordon. They informed her that the press had dubbed her "Lady Lindy" due to her resemblance to Charles Lindbergh.[3] The comparison did not please Earhart.[4]

After they had slept for five or six hours, the three fliers awoke to dozens of congratulatory telegrams. One was from President Calvin Coolidge:

> TO YOU THE FIRST WOMAN SUCCESSFULLY TO SPAN THE NORTH ATLANTIC BY AIR THE GREAT ADMIRATION OF MYSELF AND THE UNITED STATES . . .[5]

Earhart replied to the president's message stating that the flight's success "was entirely due to the great navigational skill of pilot Wilmer Stultz."[6]

Later that morning, the three flyers refueled the *Friendship* and headed for Southampton, a seaport on the coast of England. There they were greeted by Amy Guest, her son Raymond, and local officials. This was the first time Earhart had met Guest. Since the press was still hounding Earhart, Guest graciously invited her to stay at her Park Lane (London) home where she would have some privacy.

After the Friendship *flight, Amelia Earhart was greeted in Southampton, England, by Mrs. Foster Welch, the mayor of the town.*

Earhart was grateful for Guest's hospitality. She needed a female friend who would help guide her to shops where she could buy feminine clothes and accessories. The three days she had planned to stay in England had been extended to ten. She received many invitations from women's clubs and flying groups who wished to honor her.

Displeased that she was receiving all the attention after the flight, Earhart continually referred to herself as "a sack of potatoes, a back-seat driver, a dead-head passenger."[7] As far as she was concerned, Stultz and Gordon deserved all the credit. All she did was tag along for moral support and to "take pictures of the clouds."[8]

At a luncheon given for Earhart by the women's section of the Air League of the British Empire, she met Lady Mary Heath. Lady Heath was one of Britain's foremost women pilots. She had just recently flown her airplane, an Avro Avian Moth, from Capetown, South Africa, to London, England. The two women had a lot in common. The next morning Earhart met Lady Heath at the Croydon Airport. They took a short flight in Lady Heath's Avro. Earhart liked the plane so much that when Lady Heath mentioned she was going to sell it, Earhart asked if Heath would trust her for the price of the plane. Lady Heath agreed to the arrangement.

Shopping

When Amy Guest took Amelia Earhart shopping at a Mayfair department store, the owner, Gordon Selfridge, would not let Earhart pay for her purchases. No matter where she shopped, no store owner would let her pay. Also, Guest gave Earhart a handsome alligator handbag and slipped a ten-pound English note inside saying it was for her to spend on little things she might need. Earhart was overwhelmed by everyone's generosity.[9]

Two days later, Earhart along with Stultz and Gordon, left by sea for home aboard the U.S.S. *President Roosevelt*. Lady Heath's little plane was also on board. During the voyage, Earhart received a radiogram from George Putnam. Thirty-two cities had invited the *Friendship* crew to be honored in public receptions. Earhart said that if they accepted all of the invitations they "might not have got home in a year and a day."[10] Putnam, who was handling public relations for the crew, decided they should go to New York City, Boston, and Chicago.

During the cruise home, the captain of the U.S.S. *President Roosevelt*, Harry Manning, took a special interest in Earhart. Daily she went to his chart room where he plotted his ship's course. During these visits, Manning gave her lessons in navigation. Earhart confided in Manning her concerns about all the attention that was being paid her after the *Friendship* flight.

When they arrived in New York City, they received a hero's welcome. They rode through downtown perched on the backseat of a convertible and waved to the huge crowds of spectators. From the buildings above them, ticker tape and pages from telephone books were thrown down on them. Earhart found great humor in the situation. "Riding up Main Street while people throw telephone books at you is an amusing modern version of a triumphal march," she said.[11]

The crew of the *Friendship* flight received a similar reception in Boston. In Chicago, Bill Stultz disappeared just before they were about to ride in the parade to city hall. Earhart and Gordon wanted to cancel but George Putnam convinced them not to.

Amelia Earhart was greeted as a celebrity in New York City after the Friendship *flight.*

He opened Stultz's suitcase, took out his leather flying helmet, and put it on his head. Putnam said that Chicago had been fooled before and one more time would not make a difference. Disguised as Stultz, Putnam rode in the parade to city hall where the festivities were cut short due to the heat and it was decided that Earhart would speak briefly for all three crewmembers. No one even questioned why a pilot would be wearing his helmet on a hot day in July so far away from his airplane.

Book Contract

Earhart had agreed to write a book about the *Friendship* flight for G. P. Putnam and Sons, George Putnam's publishing firm. By the end of July, she was a houseguest of the Putnams in their Rye, New York, home and pounding out her book. She chose the title of her book from Stultz's last log entry, *20 Hrs., 40 Mins.* Within two weeks she had completed the book and dedicated it to her hostess, George Putnam's wife Dorothy.[12]

Vagabond Journey

By the time Earhart finished writing her book, the Avian she had purchased from Lady Heath had been uncrated and flown to Rye. She spent several weeks correcting proofs of her book and learning to fly the Avian. During this time, she collected a "lovely

assortment of maps" and made plans to fly solo across the United States to Los Angeles, where the National Air Races were being held.[13] The flight was to be a much-needed vacation and she called it her "vagabond" journey.[14]

She left Rye, New York, on Friday, August 31, 1928, and arrived at Mines Field in Los Angeles on September 14, the seventh day of the National Air Races. Fliers were still straggling in from their cross-country journey. When she landed, the crowd gave her a standing ovation.

While attending the air show, Earhart looked over the planes on the field. They were the latest models and the best the aviation industry had to offer at the time. Compared to them, she thought her little Avian looked like a toy, a plane for an amateur. She did not intend to be an amateur for long. If she was going to pursue a career in aviation, she needed a more modern airplane.

A few days later, Earhart flew as a passenger to San Francisco and visited the Army's 381st Aero Squadron at Cressey Field. She was presented a token of their appreciation, the silver pilot's wings of the U.S. Air Service. Earhart prized this gift. Throughout her life, she often wore the wings, even on formal gowns.[15] In October, Earhart flew cross-country back to New York. By the time she arrived on October 16, she had traveled fifty-five hundred

miles and was the first woman to fly solo across the continent and back.

Lecture Tour

To promote Earhart's book, George Putnam, who was now her manager, arranged a grueling cross-country lecture tour for Earhart. In those pretelevision times, the lecture circuit was the best way for an author to gain exposure. For several months, she traveled cross-country, appearing in a different town every night, "talking aviation."[16] She became one of the most popular women in America.

Although Earhart was a good speaker, Putnam advised her on how to improve her image. He told her to talk directly into a microphone, avoid lowering her voice at the end of a sentence, and smile with her mouth closed so that the space between her front teeth did not show. He also told her that her hats were "a public menace."[17] From that point on Earhart rarely wore a hat in public. Her short tousled curls became part of her enduring image.

Aviation Editor

Near the end of her lecture tour, Earhart was offered a position as an associate editor for *Cosmopolitan* magazine. Her assignment was to write an article on aviation for each issue of the magazine. Earhart made New York City her base of operations and

moved into a tiny office. One of the first things she did when setting up her office was to circle her deadline, the fourth day of each month, on her calendar. George Putnam teased her about her long-range approach. Earhart told him that writing on a schedule frightened her and that "she would rather fly than write."[18]

Sister's Wedding

On June 29, 1929, Earhart's sister, Muriel, married Albert Morrissey in the Grace Episcopal Church, in Medford, a suburb of Boston, Massachusetts. Earhart was the maid of honor. After the ceremony the minister, Revered Dwight Hadley, asked Earhart how she felt about flying across the Atlantic aboard the *Friendship*. Earhart said she thought her sister had displayed more courage by getting married that day "than my flying did."[19]

<table><tr><td>8</td></tr></table>

QUEEN OF
THE AIR

I flew the Atlantic because I wanted to.[1]

—Amelia Earhart

In 1929, it was announced that a women's air race would be held in conjunction with the National Air Races and Aeronautical Exposition. The race would be the first one of its kind ever held and a true test of women pilots' navigational and piloting skills. Thousands of dollars of prize money was being put together. Amelia Earhart was delighted and called the opportunity, "A chance to play the game as men play it, by rules established for them as flyers, not as women."[2]

To participate in the race Earhart needed a more modern airplane. On July 30, she sold her Avian and purchased a Lockheed Vega. In the late 1920s and early 1930s, the Vega was considered the hottest plane around. It was fast and could go long distances without refueling.

The race was officially called the Women's Transcontinental Air Derby. Humorist Will Rogers called it the "Powder Puff Derby" and the name stuck despite the women pilots' objections. The nine-day race began on August 24 in Santa Monica, California, and proceeded across the United States. The women pilots made overnight stops in San Bernardino, California; Phoenix, Arizona; El Paso, Texas; Abilene, Kansas; Dallas, Texas; Wichita,

Pictured are ten of the women pilots who flew in the Women's Transcontinental Air Derby. From left to right are: Mary von Mach, Maude Keith Miller, Gladys O'Donnell, Thea Rasche, Phoebe Omlie, Louise Thaden, Amelia Earhart, Ruth Elder, Blanche Noyes, and Vera Dawn Walker.

Kansas; St. Louis, Missouri; and Columbus, Ohio. The first pilot to arrive in Cleveland won the race.

Nineteen women participated in the air derby and sixteen completed the race. They attracted large crowds, predominately women, at the airfields when they made their overnight stops. A crowd of twenty thousand waited at the airfield at Columbus, Ohio, the next-to-the-last stop in the race.

The first pilot to complete the race in Cleveland was Louise Thaden from Pittsburgh. She won $3,600 in prize money. Gladys O'Donnell from Long Beach, California, came in second and won $1,950. Even though she had the fastest plane, Earhart came in third. Her share of the prize money was $875.

Ninety-Nines

During the grueling pace of the air derby, the women pilots began talking about forming an organization that would promote women pilots and aviation. After arriving in Cleveland, Earhart, Gladys O'Donnell, Ruth Nichols, Blanche Noyes, Phoebe Omlie, and Louise Thaden met under the grandstand and discussed how to go about forming such a group.

They decided to solicit the aid of Clara Studer, head of the women's department of the Curtiss Flying Service in Long Island. She also wrote a weekly newsletter for women pilots. Studer sent a letter to 117 licensed women pilots in the United States, asking them to support and help form an organization for women pilots. Eighty-six women responded positively to the letter.

On November 2, 1929, twenty-six female pilots met at Curtiss-Wright Airfield to form the new organization. They agreed that the basic goal would be "to provide a close relationship among women pilots and to unite them in any movement that may be for their benefit or for that of aviation in general."[3] An active pilot's license would be the only requirement for membership.

The big question was what to call the group. Such names as Angels' Club, Climbing Vines, Sky Larks, Noisy Birdwomen, Homing Pigeons, and Gadflies were suggested. These names were put aside when Earhart and Jean Davis Hoyt suggested that the organization be named after the total number of charter members. First, the group was called the Seventy-Sixes, then the Eighty-Sixes, and finally the Ninety-Nines when the final tally of charter members was reached and the group incorporated.

Putnam's Divorce

In December 1929, after eighteen years of marriage, Dorothy Putnam went to Reno, Nevada, and sued her husband, George Putnam, for a divorce. In

Nevada, divorces could be obtained quickly. It was a friendly parting, neither one of them wanted any unpleasant publicity. They made an agreement out of court to share equal custody of their two sons. The divorce was final one month later, and Dorothy immediately married Captain Frank Upton.

Father's Death

Edwin Earhart continued to practice law in California after he divorced his wife. He had purchased a rustic cabin in the mountains near Los Angeles and remarried. Often his neighbors and fellow church members would ask his legal advice, but he could not bring himself to send a bill to his friends.

Earhart made numerous flights between New York and Los Angeles and often visited her father and stepmother. In the spring of 1930, she realized that her father's health was deteriorating rapidly. He confided in her that he was "long on friends, but short on cash."[4] He was worried about making his mortgage payments. Earhart paid off the two-thousand-dollar mortgage on his property to ease his mind. Several months later, on September 23, 1930, Edwin Earhart died from cancer. After his death, Earhart wired her sister back east, "Dad's last big case settled out of court, peacefully and without pain."[5]

Marriage

After George Putnam and his wife divorced, his friendship with Earhart blossomed. When he proposed the first time, she declined. She told a close friend she was "still unsold on marriage" and compared it to "a cage" that she would not be interested in until she was "unfit to work or fly."[6]

In 1931, Earhart gave in. She finally had to admit to herself that she was in love with him. She later wrote, "I couldn't continue telling myself that what I felt for GP was only friendship. I knew I had found the one person who could put up with me."[7]

They were married on Saturday, February 7, 1931, in Putnam's mother's home in Noank, Connecticut. Just before the judge arrived to perform the ceremony, Earhart handed Putnam a letter she had penciled in longhand the night before. In the letter she reminded him of her reluctance to marry and asked him to make what she called "a cruel promise" that he would let her go in a year if they did not find "happiness together."[8]

After reading the letter, Putnam nodded in agreement to her terms and the wedding proceeded. The ceremony took only five minutes and was witnessed by Mrs. Frances Putnam, Putnam's mother; the judge; the judge's son; and two black cats. Putnam wore a business suit and Earhart wore a simple brown suit with a crepe blouse. After the

Amelia Earhart and George Putnam stroll arm in arm shortly after their marriage in 1931.

ceremony, the couple left for an undisclosed location. They were both back in New York, working at their desks, two days later. After her marriage, Earhart continued to use her own last name. At the time, this was an uncommon thing for a married woman to do.

Flight Across the Atlantic

One morning, in January 1932, while eating breakfast with her husband, Earhart lowered the morning newspaper and asked, "Would you mind if I flew the Atlantic?"[9] Putnam was not averse to the idea as long as Earhart felt she was ready to attempt the flight. As her manager and publicist, he knew that aviation celebrities had to continually set new records to keep their names in the news. By flying across the Atlantic again, she would set two new world records. She would be the first woman to fly solo across the Atlantic and the first person to cross the Atlantic "twice in a heavier than-air craft."[10]

In the five years since Charles Lindbergh's historic flight, eight pilots had crossed the Atlantic, but none of them had flown solo. Four pilots with partners had attempted the flight and died. Two other pilots had attempted to fly alone and disappeared. Earhart knew the flight was dangerous, but she felt she could succeed where others had failed with "meticulous planning and total concentration."[11]

Absolute secrecy was necessary while Earhart prepared for the flight. Only two other people besides her husband knew about her plans. They were Bernt Balchen, an Arctic flyer and transatlantic pilot who had worked for Commander Byrd, and Edward "Eddie" Gorski, a master mechanic. If any newspaper reporters came snooping around, they would be led to believe that the plane was intended for one of Byrd's arctic flights.

Balchen and Gorski strengthened the fuselage of Earhart's plane so that it could accommodate additional fuel tanks. They also installed a new Pratt & Whitney Wasp engine and added additional navigational instruments. The weather over the Atlantic could be treacherous, and Earhart might have to fly blind using only instruments for long periods.

While her airplane was being overhauled, Earhart began writing her second book, *The Fun of It: Random Records of My Own Flying And of Women in Aviation.* She wanted to share her joy of flying and encourage more women to join her in the air. By the time winter turned into spring, Earhart was ready to make her transatlantic flight and had completed all but the last chapter of her new book.

Weather conditions during the first part of May were not favorable for attempting the flight. Doc Kimball, the New York weatherman who was regarded by many pilots as their most reliable advisor, was consulted regularly at the United States Weather Bureau. On Friday morning, May 19, the weather broke and Kimball predicted that the weather across the Atlantic looked good, but the slot would not last for long.

Around noon, Earhart received word from her husband in New York City that the weather conditions looked favorable. She was at the Teterboro Airport in New Jersey where her plane was housed. After discussing the weather report with Balchen and Gorski, they decided the flight was a "go." They would leave in three hours.

Earhart immediately drove to her home in Rye, New York, and changed into her flying clothes, packed her leather flying suit, and grabbed her maps and other essentials. Her husband reached the airport in time to see her off. He gave her a twenty-dollar bill and asked her to call him as soon as she landed in Europe.

At 3:15 P.M., they took off. In order to give Earhart a chance to rest, Balchen flew the plane to St. John, New Brunswick in Canada. They landed at 6:45 P.M. The next morning, Balchen flew the plane to Harbour Grace, Newfoundland. Earhart rested for a few hours, and at 7:12 P.M. she took the controls of her plane, waved good-bye to Balchen and Gorski, and took off on her solo journey across the Atlantic Ocean.

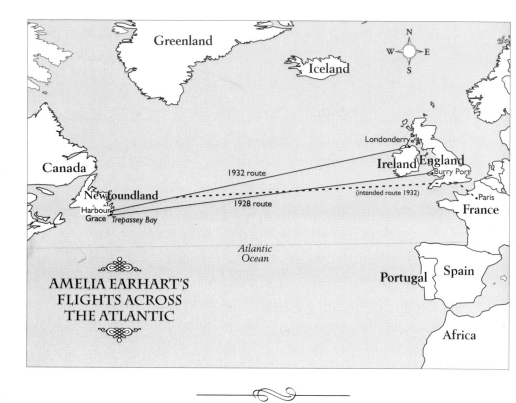

Amelia Earhart's flights across the Atlantic made her a national hero.

After traveling 2,026 miles in fourteen hours and fifty-six minutes, Earhart landed in Culmore, on the outskirts of Londonderry, Ireland, on Saturday morning, May 21, 1932. Several hours later, after receiving his wife's phone call, George Putnam announced to the world over Columbia Broadcasting's radio station, WABC, that he "just had the pleasure and the thrill and the fun and the joy" of speaking to his wife on the telephone. She was sitting "in the home of a hospitable couple in the far north of Ireland."[12]

Later in the day congratulations began to come pouring in. One of the first messages to reach Earhart was from President Herbert Hoover. He told her that she was "the pride of the nation" and that she had demonstrated her "own dauntless courage, but also the capacity of women to match the skill of men in carrying through the most difficult feats of high adventure."[13]

Honors

On May 22, Earhart flew to London. Her Vega was flown to London, where it was put on display at Selfridge's department store. While in London, Earhart visited the Prince of Wales. The Prince was fascinated with flying and prolonged her visit for over a half hour in order to hear all the details of her flight. Before she left Great Britain for France, she

received the Certificate of Honorary Membership in the British Guild of Airpilots and Navigators.

Putnam met his wife in Paris, France, on June 3. When he arrived, he told the press, "I'm terribly proud of her." Then he added, "I hope transatlantic flying won't become a habit with her."[14]

In Paris, the French Senate voted to receive Earhart in its chamber. She was the first woman from a foreign country they had chosen to honor in this way. Before she left Paris, Minister of Air Paul Painlevé presented Earhart with the Cross of Knight of the Legion of Honor. The medal is the highest honor awarded in France for outstanding services. During the presentation at the U.S. Embassy, Painleve announced that five years ago he had "the great pleasure to decorate Colonel Lindbergh after his remarkable flight. And now I have the honor to bestow this cross upon the Colonel's charming image."[15]

Next, Earhart and Putnam went to Rome, Italy, to attend a meeting of worldwide ocean pilots. Then they went to Belgium where Earhart was awarded the Cross of Chevalier of the Order of Leopold, for meritorious achievements, by King Albert. On June 15, they headed home aboard the ocean liner *Ile de France*. As the ocean liner left the harbor, three airplanes dropped flowers on the deck of the ship as a farewell to Earhart.

Welcome Home

While aboard the *Ile de France*, Earhart wired New York City Mayor James Walker, asking him to cancel all welcoming ceremonies and donate the money that would have been used to honor her to relieve unemployment in the city due to the depression. Walker refused. He felt that Earhart's flight across the Atlantic proved that American courage could overcome tremendous odds. Earhart was a symbol of hope at a time when 10 million Americans were unemployed. She was an American hero when Americans needed one most.

When the ocean liner docked in New York City on June 20, Earhart was greeted with an over-whelming welcome. Thousands of New Yorkers

The Great Depression

The Great Depression hit like a bomb after a period of tremendous prosperity. The first sign of trouble was the stock market crash in October 1929. Three years later, at least 12 million people were unemployed, one out of every four workers. Farmers were also hurt by the decline in business activity. Many farmers lost their land because they could not pay their property taxes. It was a never-ending circle of despair. People were so poor they could not buy manufactured goods. Since manufacturers could not sell their products, they laid off workers.

lined Broadway to see her. She rode in an open car and a blizzard of ticker tape surrounded her. This time the parade was for her alone.

The next day Earhart and Putnam flew to Washington, D.C., where President Herbert Hoover presented her with the National Geographic Society's Gold Medal for her contribution to the science of aviation. While in Washington, D.C., she was also awarded the Distinguished Flying Cross by

President Herbert Hoover presents the gold medal of the National Geographic Society to Amelia Earhart for recognition of her nonstop solo flight across the Atlantic Ocean in 1932.

the U.S. Congress. The flying cross is awarded to individuals who have made extraordinary achievements in aviation. Earhart was the first woman in history to receive the award.

The Fun of It

The Fun of It was published shortly after Earhart returned from Europe. She had written the final chapter about her transatlantic flight after arriving in Great Britain and cabled it to her publisher in New York. George Putnam guaranteed his wife's book would be a best-seller by making sure it came out during the media blitz following Earhart's flight. The first edition of the book included a recording of a speech Earhart gave in London over transatlantic radio.

Earhart spent many months lecturing around the country and promoting her new book. Her lecture tour was like walking on a treadmill, lecture after lecture, day after day. Sometimes she would give three or four lectures a day. Then she would get back into her car and drive until midnight to the next stop.

Amelia Earhart Design

On one of her lecture tours, Earhart met a luggage designer. While talking with him, she mentioned ways in which she felt luggage could be made more

practical for air travel. The designer asked her to write down her ideas. This led Earhart to an association with Orenstein Trunk Corporation of Newark, New Jersey. The company began producing Amelia Earhart Air-Light Luggage. They advertised the luggage as "the first truly practical and genuine airplane luggage."[16] It weighed one third less than previous travel luggage and was an immediate success.

Next, Earhart tried her hand at designing clothes for active women. Her tailored creations were marketed under the label "Amelia Earhart Design" and were popular with professional women and businesswomen. They were designed for comfort and inspired by aviation. "I tried to put the freedom that is in flying into the clothes. And the efficiency too," Earhart said.[17]

She used parachute silk for blouses and fashioned buttonholes and fasteners in the shape of airplane hardware. Unfortunately, her endeavor was not long lived. She insisted on using the best materials, which made her clothes expensive. Her costly line of clothes was forced out of the marketplace by competitors with cheaper prices within a year.

9

FLIGHTS AND MORE FLIGHTS

Ours is the commencement of a flying age and I am happy to have popped into existence at a period so interesting.[1]

—Amelia Earhart

A t the age of thirty-six, Amelia Earhart had a decision to make. Should she disappear from the public eye into semiretirement, as Charles Lindbergh had done? Or, should she continue to be a trailblazer and make more pioneering flights? She chose the latter. In August 1932, she set a women's nonstop transcontinental speed record for flying from Los Angeles, California, to Newark, New Jersey, in nineteen hours and five minutes. The following summer she broke her previous record.

She flew the same route in seventeen hours and seven-and-a-half minutes.

Flight Across the Pacific

Next, she turned her attention to the Pacific Ocean. A few pilots with crews had flown over the Pacific Ocean. But no one, neither a man nor a woman, had flown solo. The flight was one of the few firsts left for a pilot to achieve.

One autumn evening in 1933, Earhart announced to her husband, as he was returning home from work, that she wanted "to fly the Pacific soon."[2] He asked her if she meant from San Francisco to Honolulu. She replied that she wanted to make the flight the other way around, from Honolulu to San Francisco. Then she jokingly added, "it's easier to hit a continent than an island."[3] He asked when she wanted to make the flight. She replied soon but only when she was ready.

Following her husband's advice, Earhart hired Paul Mantz as her technical advisor for the flight. Mantz was an excellent pilot. He had masterminded the aerial stunts and dogfights in the movie *Wings*. Putnam had been associated with the film, which, in 1927–1928, was the first movie to win an Academy Award for best picture. (Academy awards were given every two years until 1934.)

In order to make the flight, Earhart's new Vega, which she had recently purchased from another woman pilot, would have to be overhauled and outfitted with a two-way radio. To cover the expensive preparations, Putnam arranged for a group of Hawaiian businessmen to sponsor the flight. Amelia Earhart would receive five thousand dollars initially. She would get another five thousand dollars after successfully completing the flight.

On December 22, Earhart, Putnam, Paul Mantz and his wife Myrtle, and Ernie Tissot, Earhart's mechanic, left for Honolulu aboard the *Lurline*. Earhart's Vega was strapped to the deck of the ship. Several times during their five-day journey across the Pacific, they started up the airplane's motor to prevent it from being corroded by the moist sea air. While the motor was running, they were able to pick up and communicate with radio stations as far away as Kingman, Arizona.

When they arrived in Honolulu, the announcement of Earhart's plan to fly across the Pacific was met by a round of criticism. The *Oakland Tribune* declared that her proposed flight was "extremely hazardous, valueless to aviation if it succeeds and a costly setback if it fails."[4] The Honolulu *Star-Bulletin* claimed that Army airmen were "uneasy" about Earhart flying across the Pacific.[5] The airmen lacked confidence in a female pilot. Then the U.S.

Navy refused to clear her flight. The Navy claimed that Earhart's radio "lacked sufficient range for safety."[6]

On January 2, Earhart gave a speech at the University of Hawaii's Farrington Hall. While she spoke, Paul Mantz took her airplane up to twelve thousand feet over Honolulu. During the flight, he made two-way contact with several mainland radio stations. Shortly afterward, the Navy regrouped and cleared Earhart's flight.

Earhart planned to take off on January 11, but it was raining "like a waterfall."[7] By 3:30 P.M., it had stopped raining and she decided to check out the grass airstrip at Wheeler Field where her plane was stored. To aid Earhart in taking off, the Army had mowed the six-thousand-foot airstrip and marked it off with white distance flags on both sides. Even though the airstrip was solid mud, Mantz felt she could get her plane safely in the air within three thousand feet. Future weather conditions looked bad. Earhart feared that if she did not take off that afternoon, her flight might be delayed indefinitely.

At 4:30 P.M., Earhart climbed into her cockpit and began warming up the motor. Only a few hundred people were at the airfield to watch her start her journey. It was a somber group. Their spirits had been dampened by the rain. While her gear was being stowed on the plane, she noted that "several women with handkerchiefs obviously ready for an emergency" were standing nearby and "three fire engines and an ambulance" were posted near the end of the field.[8] It appeared to her that all the Army men present "seemed to have portable fire extinguishers in their hands," prepared for the worst.[9]

Earhart did not let the somber mood at the airstrip affect her. She asked the men on the field to remove the blocks in front of the wheels of her plane. Then she began to taxi to the airstrip. Her mechanic Ernie Tissot ran alongside her plane, splashing mud all over his shoes. She noted that "his face was as white as paper" and she wanted to call out to him and tell him to cheer up. But, she knew he could not hear her.[10]

When she was lined up at the airstrip for take off, she realized that the wind was with her. That was to her disadvantage. She later wrote that a plane needed to "take off against the wind, not with it, just as a small boy flies a kite. He doesn't run with the wind to get his kite in the air, but runs against it. Of course an airplane is simply a kite with a motor instead of a small boy."[11]

Earhart pushed the throttle forward. Her plane started to gather speed as it rolled down the airstrip. Then at two thousand feet, she hit a bump that bounced the plane up into the air. She pushed her throttle forward to its highest notch and was off.

Flying out over Honolulu, Earhart noted that she "could see the human ants, far below, going home after their day's work."[12] She climbed to eight thousand feet and leveled off. An hour into her flight she transmitted a message stating everything was okay. Earhart's flight was the first civilian long-distance flight made with a two-way radio.

Eighteen hours and sixteen minutes later, she landed in Oakland, California. Her plane performed perfectly. She later wrote that her night over the Pacific "was a night of stars. They seemed to rise from the sea and hang outside my cockpit window, near enough to touch, until hours later they slipped away into the dawn."[13]

Mexican Journey

A few months after Earhart's flight across the Pacific, she was invited by the president of Mexico to make a goodwill flight to his country. To help finance the flight, the Mexican government agreed to issue a limited edition of a commemorative stamp with a message that translated as "Amelia Earhart Good-Will Flight Mexico, 1935" printed across it.[14] Of the 780 stamps printed, George Putnam purchased 300. They were autographed by Earhart, and later sold to stamp collectors.

On the evening of April 19, 1935, Earhart took off from the Burbank Airport in California, headed for Mexico City. During the evening, she enjoyed the moonlight over Baja and the Gulf of California. When she reached Mazatlan, she headed east toward the Mexican capital.

After nearly ten hours in the air, she realized that "there was a railroad beneath" her and that a railroad "had no business being" there if she were on course.[15] While she was examining her maps, a small insect or speck of dirt flew into one of her eyes. It was "extremely painful" and "played havoc" with her sight. Then her other eye "went on strike in sympathy with its ailing mate."[16] Unable to read anything, Earhart decided to land in a dry riverbed. She hoped to figure things out after she landed.

The local villagers tried to be helpful but none of them spoke English, and Earhart did not speak Spanish. One enterprising young lad was able to make Earhart understand where she was by pointing to his village on one of her maps. She was in Nopala, about fifty miles from Mexico City.

A half hour later, Earhart took off again. She landed at the Valbuena Airport in Mexico City, slightly over thirteen hours after beginning her flight. She had flown seventeen hundred miles but was disappointed that she had not been able to fly nonstop. A crowd of spectators met her at the airport, including her husband and Foreign Minister

Emilio Portes Gil, who presented her with a bouquet of flowers.

From Mexico City, Earhart planned to fly to New York. Due to the weather, her flight was delayed until the morning of May 8, 1935. It was a dangerous takeoff due to the high 7,200-foot elevation of Mexico City and the weight of her plane, which was burdened with 470 gallons of fuel. At 6:10 A.M., it took all of Earhart's skill as a pilot and every inch of the extended runway for her to take off. The rest of her journey was uneventful, for flying conditions were ideal that day. Fourteen hours and nineteen minutes later, she landed at the Newark airport. She had traveled 2,185 miles, and later she wrote, "All in all, the fight was marked by a delightful precision. Everything worked as it should."[17]

When Earhart landed in Newark, the crowd overran the field. As she climbed down from the cockpit, two husky policemen tried to escort her to safety. One grabbed her right arm and the other her left leg. Even though their intentions were good, their efforts lacked coordination. One pulled her in one direction and the other, the opposite. Earhart wrote about her experience, comparing it to being exposed to the "tortures of the rack."[18]

Purdue University

After her flight to Mexico City, Earhart was honored at a dinner sponsored by the Mexican government in New York City. At the dinner, she met Edward C. Elliott, the president of Purdue University in Lafayette, Indiana. Purdue was a coeducational university with approximately five thousand male and one thousand female students. Elliott asked Earhart to become a career counselor for women at the university. He also wanted her to provide technical advice to their Department of Aeronautics. Purdue was ahead of the times. They were one of the few universities in the world with an aviation department and their own landing field. On June 2, 1935, Earhart accepted the position and became a visiting faculty member with a salary of two thousand dollars per academic year.

Earhart spent several weeks each term in residence at the university. She stayed in the women's residence hall and counseled women students individually, lectured, and in general, tried to "improve the climate for women on the campus."[19]

Sometimes Putnam stayed with his wife in the women's dormitory. She often told students about his belief that wives should do "what they do best" and that he was "an approving and helpful partner in all" her projects.[20]

Unconventional Behavior

At Purdue, Earhart often showed her independence by putting her elbows on the table during meals or showing up for dinner wearing her flying clothes in the women's dining hall. When students tried to follow Earhart's example and bend the rules, the housemother would tell them, "As soon as you fly the Atlantic, you may!"[21]

One day President Elliott asked Putnam what interested his wife "beyond immediate academic matters." Putnam replied "a bigger and better airplane. Not only to go to far places further and faster and more safely but essentially for pioneering in aviation education and technical experimentation."[22] Elliott liked the idea and put into motion the necessary academic and financial arrangements to make it possible. On April 19, 1936, Purdue announced the establishment of the Amelia Earhart Fund for Aeronautical Research. The fund was set up to supply Earhart with a brand-new airplane and funds to pursue her goals of long-distance flying.

AROUND THE WORLD

I think I have just one more long flight left in my system.[1]

—Amelia Earhart

On July 21, 1936, Amelia Earhart took her new Lockheed Electra 10E out for a test flight. The twin-engine, all-metal monoplane was the "big brother" to the two Lockheed Vegas she previously owned.[2] Three days later, on Earhart's thirty-ninth birthday, she took possession of the plane. She was so pleased, she told Lockheed mechanics, "I could write poetry about this ship."[3]

The Electra had a wingspan of fifty-five feet, was nearly thirty-nine feet long, could fly to an altitude of nineteen thousand feet, and had a range of four

Amelia Earhart (on top of plane) poses with students from Indiana's Purdue University at the college's airstrip with her brand new Lockheed Electra 10E.

thousand miles. The plane was equipped with a two-way radio with a long trailing wire antenna and a Morse code transmitting key. Earhart now had the communication equipment she needed to attempt her next challenge. She planned to fly around the world.

Preparations for the Flight

Earhart believed that preparation was two thirds of any successful venture. Flying around the world required a great deal more planning than her previous flights had. Thousands of details had to be attended to before the flight.

Maps had to be collected and her course meticulously plotted. Permission to enter and land an aircraft in the countries on her route had to be obtained. In addition, fuel and replacement parts needed to be stored along her route.

In announcing her flight to reporters, Earhart said she would fly twenty-seven thousand miles around the center of the world, following the equator. She planned to fly during the day and stop at

Amelia Earhart inspects the equipment in her airplane.

designated airports or landing strips at night. Earhart would begin her record-breaking flight from Oakland, California, and fly twenty-four hundred miles across the Pacific Ocean to Oahu, Hawaii. Then from Hawaii, she would fly eighteen hundred miles to Howland Island in the South Pacific.

According to Earhart, Howland Island was a "fantastically tiny target" with dimensions of less than one mile by two miles.[4] Because of this, she chose to take along two navigators, Fred Noonan and Captain Harry Manning. Noonan was a pilot and an expert in celestial navigation. He was also rumored to be a heavy drinker. Evidently, Earhart was not aware of the rumors or did not believe them. Manning was an expert in Morse code. Earhart had met him in 1928, after the *Friendship* flight. She had returned to New York aboard his ship, U.S.S. *President Roosevelt*.

Journey Begins

On the afternoon of March 17, 1937, Earhart took off from Oakland, California, headed for Hawaii. On board were Paul Mantz, her technical advisor, and her two navigators. It was St. Patrick's Day and Earhart gave everyone shamrocks to wear for good luck.[5] The two navigators sat in the back of the plane where a small worktable had been installed for them. They communicated with Earhart and Mantz

Navigation

Navigation is the process of determining an airplane's position and directing its movements. The word *navigate* originates from two Greek words meaning "ship" and "drive." In the 1930s, pilots used several methods to navigate their airplanes: piloting, dead reckoning, celestial, and radio navigation.

In piloting, a pilot used landmarks to determine his location and course.

Dead reckoning was used when there were few or no landmarks and involved estimating an airplane's position by taking into account how far and in what direction the plane was traveling.

Celestial navigation determined an airplane's location in relationship to celestial bodies—the sun, moon, stars, and planets. Once the position of the plane was determined with a tool called a sextant, an almanac would be consulted that listed the positions of celestial bodies at all times of the year.

Radio navigation involves using radio signals to determine the location of an airplane in relationship to the radio station emitting the signals.

in the cockpit by passing notes attached to a modified bamboo fishing pole with a clip on one end to hold the messages. Fifteen hours and fifty-two and a half minutes after takeoff, they landed in Wheeler Field in Honolulu, Hawaii. The flight set a new speed record for traveling east to west from Oakland to Honolulu.

On March 19, Earhart's Electra was moved to Luke Field, a Navy airstrip near Pearl Harbor. Luke Field had a longer and better-surfaced runway. It was decided that Mantz would stay in Hawaii and Manning and Noonan would accompany Earhart across the Pacific. At dawn the following day, Earhart attempted to take off. Everything was going smoothly and then the Electra suddenly pulled to the right. "I reduced the power on the opposite engine and succeeded in swinging from the right to the left," Earhart wrote about the incident. She continued:

> For a moment I thought I would be able to gain control and straighten the course. But, alas, the load was so heavy, once it started an arc there were nothing to do but let the plane ground loop as easily as possible . . . the landing gear on the right was wrenched free and gasoline sprayed from the drain-well. . . .[6]

Earhart stayed calm and immediately after the crash turned off the ignition to prevent a fire.

After the crash, Earhart vowed to attempt the flight again. At noon, she boarded the U.S.S. *Malolo* and sailed home to the United States. A week later, her Electra was shipped to the Lockheed factory in Burbank, California. The verdict from the Lockheed mechanics was that the Electra would take five weeks to repair at a cost of $25,000. She also needed another $25,000 to rearrange the flight. Concerning the situation, Amelia said, "I am more or less mortgaging my future to go on. But what are futures for?"[7]

Due to weather conditions, Earhart decided to change her route and fly east to west. This time Paul Mantz and Fred Manning would not be involved with the flight. George Putnam was evidently unhappy with Mantz. The two men supposedly argued about money. Manning's leave was up, and he had returned to his ship.

Once again, Earhart would start her journey from Oakland, California. On the afternoon of March 21, 1937, she took off. Accompanying her were her husband, Fred Noonan, and Bo McKneeley, her flight mechanic. They flew to Tucson, Arizona, refueled, and headed for New Orleans, Louisiana, where they spent the night. The following day they reached Miami, Florida. Earhart spent over a week in Miami making the final preparations for her flight and checking out her airplane.

On the morning of June 1, she took off from Miami heading for San Juan, Puerto Rico, with only Fred Noonan aboard. From Puerto Rico, they spent three days flying over South America. From Natal, Brazil, they crossed the Atlantic Ocean and landed on St. Louis Island on the Senegal River delta in northwest Africa, on June 7. It took them eight days to fly across Africa to Karachi, Pakistan. From each stop, Earhart cabled articles about her flight to the *New York Herald Tribune*. She hoped to turn the articles into a book after her successful flight.

In Karachi, Earhart telephoned her husband. Putnam asked how she was feeling and she replied, "Swell! Never better."[8] Then he asked whether she was having a good time and she replied, "You betja! It's a grand trip. We'll do it again, together, some-time."[9]

Next, Earhart and Noonan flew to Calcutta, India, through heavy rains. The rain was so heavy Earhart thought they might have drowned if her "cockpit hadn't been secure."[10] In Calcutta, Earhart communicated with her husband again. This time, she had alarming news. "I'm starting to have per-sonnel trouble," she said.[11] Putnam told his wife to stop the flight and not take any more chances. Earhart replied, "I have only one bad hop left and I am pretty sure I can handle the situation."[12] Friends assumed that the personnel problem was Noonan and that he had begun drinking again.

On June 21, they reached Bandoeng in the Dutch East Indies, where they stayed for five days due to engine and instrument problems. They landed in Darwin, Australia, on June 28. At dawn on June 29, they flew to Lae, New Guinea. At this point, they had flown twenty-two thousand miles around the world and had only seven thousand miles left to complete their journey.

From Lae on July 1, 1937, Earhart wrote:

Not much more than a month ago I was on the other shore of the Pacific, looking westward. This evening, I looked eastward over the Pacific. In those fast moving days which have intervened, the whole width of the world has passed behind us—except this broad ocean. I shall be glad when we have the hazards of its navigation behind us.[13]

On July 2 at 10:00 A.M., they left Lae. Observers commented that it was a "hair-raising" takeoff.[14] Earhart needed every inch of the one-thousand-yard runway to become airborne. She was only inches above the water when she came to the end of the runway. Eighteen hours later, they were expected to land on Howland Island. The Coast Guard cutter *Itasca* sat off the coast of Howland to monitor radio contact with Earhart and assist her if necessary.

The *Itasca* received several radio messages from Earhart. Many times when they responded to her messages, Earhart did not acknowledge them. It appeared she was having radio problems. Plus, there was some confusion regarding the radio frequency she would be using.

What the crew of the *Itasca* did not know was that Earhart had left her long-trailing wire radio antenna, along with her Morse code key, in Miami. Earhart disliked the antenna because she had to

crank it out every time she wanted to use it. She was also uncomfortable with Morse code. Perhaps Earhart was overconfident. She had not used any of these tools on her past flights.

Nineteen hours into the flight, Earhart radioed the *Itasca* that they were running out of gas and unable to make contact. She reported they were flying at one thousand feet. An hour and fourteen minutes later, Earhart's last message was received.

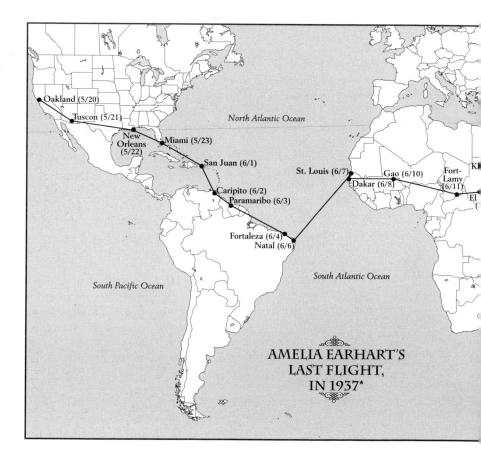

AMELIA EARHART'S
LAST FLIGHT,
IN 1937*

"WE ARE ON THE LINE OF POSITION 157- 337, WILL REPEAT THIS MESSAGE, WILL REPEAT THIS MESSAGE ON 6210 KCS. WAIT LISTEN-ING ON 6210 KSC . . . WE ARE NOW RUNNING NORTH AND SOUTH."[15]

Search

A few hours after receiving Earhart's last message, she was declared missing. A massive sea-and-air

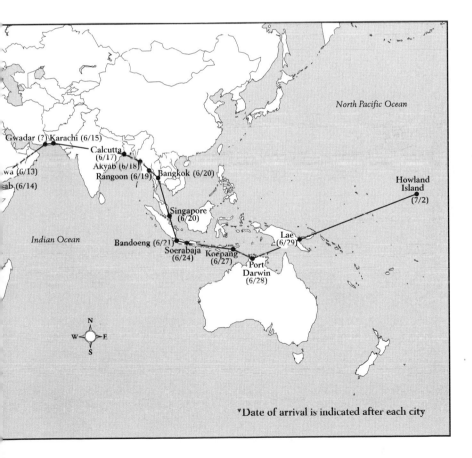

*Date of arrival is indicated after each city

search was undertaken by the U.S. Navy. Ten ships, 102 airplanes, and 3,000 men searched 220,000 square miles of the Pacific Ocean and found nothing. On July 18, 1937, after sixteen days, the Navy called off the search. Earhart and Noonan had disappeared without a trace. To this day, their fate is unknown.

11

EPILOGUE

Courage is the price that life exacts for granting peace.
The soul that knows it not, knows no release. . . .[1]
—Amelia Earhart

For several years, George Putnam used his own money to continue searching for his wife. He was the victim of many con artists who came up with schemes to steal money from him. Amy Earhart never gave up hope that one day her daughter would come home. She died, still waiting, in 1962, at the age of ninety-five.

Muriel Earhart Morrissey published a biography of her sister, *Amelia, My Courageous Sister*, in 1987. She wanted her sister to be remembered

In Memory of Amelia Earhart

The International Organization of Women Pilots, the Ninety-Nines, an organization Amelia Earhart founded, is determined to preserve Amelia Earhart's memory. They have six thousand members from thirty-five countries. Their main office and museum in Oklahoma City, Oklahoma, is located on Amelia Earhart Road. In Atchison, Kansas, they have purchased Amelia's birthplace and have turned it into a museum dedicated to her memory. Each year they award Amelia Earhart Memorial Scholarships to qualified members for advanced flight training or courses in specialized areas of aviation.

because Amelia loved flying and wanted it to be safe so that people would enjoy flying as much as she did. In her later years, Morrissey became an advocate of her sister's legacy and tried to downplay the mystery of her disappearance. She died in 1997, at the age of ninety-eight.

Disappearance Theories

Over the years, many theories have evolved concerning Earhart and Noonan's fate. Some are plausible and others are quite outlandish. At one point, Earhart's family was convinced that she was on a spy mission for the Roosevelt Administration. Both President Franklin Roosevelt and his wife denied that accusation. In fact, Eleanor Roosevelt

told Amelia's sister, "Franklin and I loved Amelia too much to send her to her death."[2]

Another theory was that Earhart and Noonan were captured by the Japanese, who thought they were spies. This theory held that Noonan was executed and Earhart was taken to Japan, where she became Tokyo Rose, the wartime radio announcer who used propaganda to attempt to persuade American troops to stop fighting. Since Tokyo Rose had a distinct New York accent, some officials thought it might be Earhart. George Putnam made a special trip to the front lines during World War II to listen to a Tokyo Rose broadcast. He set the record straight. Tokyo Rose was not Earhart.[3]

Most historians believe that Earhart's plane either ran out of fuel and plunged into the ocean or crash-landed on an island in the Pacific Ocean. Several individuals and groups are still actively trying to solve the Earhart mystery. The International Group for Historic Aircraft Recovery, TIGHAR, believes that Earhart's Electra wandered off course and landed on Nikumaroru, an uninhabited atoll in the Republic of Kiribati, in the central Pacific. (An atoll is a ring-shaped coral island surrounding a lagoon.) Nikumaroru, formerly known as Gardiner Island, is about five hundred miles south of Howland Island.

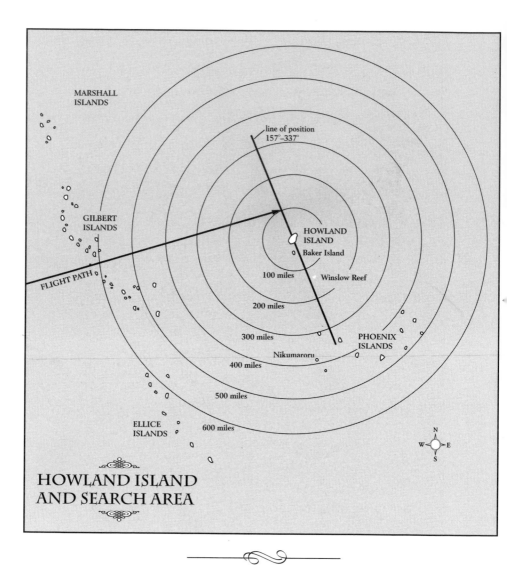

MARSHALL
ISLANDS

line of position
157°–337°

GILBERT
ISLANDS

HOWLAND
ISLAND

Baker Island

FLIGHT PATH

100 miles

Winslow Reef

200 miles

300 miles

PHOENIX
ISLANDS

Nikumaroru

400 miles

500 miles

ELLICE
ISLANDS

600 miles

N
W   E
S

HOWLAND ISLAND
AND SEARCH AREA

*Rescue and recovery teams searched a huge area around the last line
of position reported by Amelia Earhart. Earhart, Fred Noonan, and
the plane were never found.*

Richard Gillespie, a former aviation accident investigator and executive director of TIGHAR, believes that Earhart and Noonan were marooned on Nikumaroru and eventually died due to injuries, lack of water, or from eating poisonous fish that are common in that area. Since 1989, TIGHAR has spent $2 million on four expeditions to Nikumaroru and found nothing conclusive that could be traced back to Earhart, Noonan, or Earhart's airplane.

Elgen Long, a record-setting pilot who has flown solo around the world from the North Pole to the South Pole, and his wife, Marie, have spent twenty-five years investigating Amelia Earhart's last flight. They believe that Earhart's plane ran out of fuel shortly after her last radio message and plunged into the ocean. In 1999, they published a book about their theory, *Amelia Earhart: Mystery Solved*. The following year, they appeared on NBC's *Today Show* and announced that *NOVA*, the PBS science series, was interested in helping them prove their theory and documenting the expedition.

David Jourdan, the founder of a maritime exploration company called Nauticos, has also joined forces with the Longs. Jourdan's Maryland-based company has made some impressive finds in the past. In 1995, Nauticos helped find the *I-52*, a World War II Japanese submarine that was sunk by American bombers in 1944. Bound for Germany,

the submarine was carrying tin, rubber, two tons of gold bullion, and opium. Several years later, they located the *Dakar*, an Israeli submarine that had been missing for nearly thirty years, at the bottom of the Atlantic Ocean. While searching for the *Dakar*, they discovered the wreck of an ancient Greek ship dating from 300 B.C. on the floor of the Mediterranean Ocean. Nauticos has also located the wreckage of the IJN *Kaga*, a Japanese aircraft carrier that had sunk in the Battle of Midway during World War II in the Pacific Ocean.

In March 2002, Nauticos began a $1.7 million deep-sea search for Earhart's plane near Howard Island in the Pacific Ocean. Jourdan was confident that his company would be successful. "We have been able to find anything we went out to look for, no matter how deep," he told a reporter.[4] After six weeks of searching at the depth of eighteen thousand feet with a deep-sea sonar listening system attached to a thirty-three thousand-foot steel-covered fiber-optic cable, Jourdan had to give up the expedition due to equipment failure. Only two thirds of the search area designated by Long's research had been covered.

Both TIGHAR and Nauticos are considering future expeditions. Possibly someday, we will know what really happened to Amelia Earhart on her last flight. Until that time, her disappearance will remain one of the greatest mysteries of the twentieth century.

Legacy

Amelia Earhart was a free spirit who loved to fly. She was a fearless adventurer and refused to confine herself to the traditional roles for women of her time. She believed that a woman could do anything a man could do, and was a fierce crusader for women's rights.

Earhart envisioned a future where flying would be accepted as the fastest, safest, and most comfortable way of traveling anywhere on our planet. Through her efforts and beliefs, she paved the way for women to take their place in the aviation industry as fighter pilots, captains of commercial airplanes, aeronautical engineers, and astronauts. Through their achievements, Amelia Earhart's legacy lives on.

CHRONOLOGY

1897—Born in Atchison, Kansas, on July 24.

1908—Sees first airplane at the Iowa State Fair.

1918—Becomes volunteer nurse at Spadina Military Hospital in Toronto, Canada.

1919—Returns to the United States; Attends Columbia University for one semester.

1920—Parents in Los Angeles, California; Meets Sam Chapman; Goes on first airplane ride.

1921—Takes flying lessons from Neta Snook; Buys first airplane.

1922—Sets women's altitude record by flying at fourteen thousand feet.

1923—Becomes engaged to Sam Chapman.

1924—Parents divorce; Sells airplane and buys Kissel touring car; Drives back east with mother.

1926—Becomes social worker at Denison House in Boston, Massachusetts.

1928—Becomes the first woman to fly across the Atlantic Ocean as a passenger on June 17–18; Buys Avro Avian airplane; Writes book entitled *20 Hrs., 40 Min.*; Ends engagement with Sam Chapman; Becomes first woman to fly solo across the United States and back.

1929—Purchases Lockheed Vega airplane; Takes third place in first Women's Air Derby from Santa Monica, California, to Cleveland, Ohio, on August 18–22.

1930—Helps organize the Ninety-Nines, the first organization for women pilots; Father dies of cancer.

1931—Marries George Putnam on February 7.

1932—Writes second book, entitled *The Fun of It*; Becomes first woman to fly solo across the Atlantic Ocean, on May 20–21; Sets women's nonstop transcontinental speed record from Los Angeles, California, to Newark, New Jersey, on August 24–25.

1935—Flies solo from Honolulu to Oakland, California, on January 11–12; Becomes first person to fly solo from Los Angeles, California, to Mexico City, Mexico, on April 19–20; Flies solo from Mexico City to Newark, New Jersey, on May 8.

1936—Becomes career counselor at Purdue University; Takes delivery of Lockheed twin-engine airplane; Begins to plan around-the-world flight.

1937—Flies from Oakland, California, to Honolulu, Hawaii, on March 17–18 to begin around-the-world flight; Sets record traveling east to west; crashes on takeoff, headed for Howland Island on March 20; Begins around-the-world flight from Miami, Florida, on June 1; Disappears after completing twenty-two thousand miles of her flight around the world on July 2.

CHAPTER NOTES

Chapter 1. Solo Across the Atlantic

1. Amelia Earhart, *Last Flight* (New York: Crown Trade Paperbacks, 1968), p. 2.

2. Amelia Earhart, "The Society's Special Medal Awarded to Amelia Earhart Atlantic," *National Geographic*, September 1932, p. 363.

3. Amelia Earhart, *The Fun of It* (Chicago, Ill.: Academy Chicago Publishers, 1932), p. 214.

4. George Putnam, *Soaring Wings* (New York: Harcourt, Brace & Co., 1939), p. 108.

5. Earhart, "The Society's Special Medal Awarded to Amelia Earhart Atlantic," p. 365.

6. Ibid.

7. Donald M. Goldstein and Katherine V. Dillon, *Amelia: A Life of the Aviation Legend* (Washington, D.C.: Brassey's, 1999), p. 97.

Chapter 2. Early Years

1. Amelia Earhart, *The Fun of It* (Chicago, Ill.: Academy Chicago Publishers, 1932), p. 5.

2. Susan Butler, *East to the Dawn* (Reading, Mass.: Addison-Wesley, 1997), p. 20.

3. Ibid., p. 25.

4. Ibid., p. 26.

5. Mary S. Lovell, *The Sound of Wings: The Life of Amelia Earhart* (New York: St. Martin's Press, 1968), p. 9.

6. Jean L. Backus, *Letters from Amelia 1901–1937* (Boston: Beacon Press, 1982), p. 13.

7. Ibid.

8. Earhart, p. 5.

9. Butler, p. 30.

10. Ibid.

Chapter 3. Tomboy

1. Amelia Earhart, *The Fun of It* (Chicago, Ill.: Academy Chicago Publishers, 1932), p. 11.

2. Doris L. Rich, *Amelia Earhart: A Biography* (Washington, D.C.: Smithsonian Institution Press, 1989), p. 4.

3. Susan Butler, *East to the Dawn* (Reading, Mass.: Addison-Wesley, 1997), p. 41.

4. Ibid.

5. Ibid., p. 36.

6. Earhart, p. 12.

7. Muriel Earhart Morrissey and Carol L. Osborne, *Amelia, My Courageous Sister: Biography of Amelia Earhart* (Santa Clara, Calif.: Osborne Publisher, 1987), p. 11.

8. Ibid., p. 16.

9. Ibid., p. 17.

Chapter 4. Maverick

1. Susan Ware, *Still Missing: Amelia Earhart and the Search for Modern Feminism* (New York: W. W. Norton & Company, 1993), p. 30.

2. Muriel Earhart Morrissey and Carol L. Osborne, *Amelia, My Courageous Sister: Biography of Amelia Earhart* (Santa Clara, Calif.: Osborne Publisher, 1987), p. 25.

3. Mary S. Lovell, *The Sound of Wings: The Life of Amelia Earhart* (New York: St. Martin's Press, 1968), p. 15.

4. Amelia Earhart, *Last Flight* (New York: Crown Trade Paperbacks, 1968), p. 2.

5. Susan Butler, *East to the Dawn* (Reading, Mass.: Addison-Wesley, 1997), p. 49.

6. Ibid.

7. Ibid.

8. Lovell, p. 16.

9. Ibid.

10. Morrissey and Osborne, p. 40.

11. Ibid., p. 42.

Chapter 5. First Flight

1. Amelia Earhart, *The Fun of It* (Chicago, Ill.: Academy Chicago Publishers, 1932), p. 25.

2. Muriel Earhart Morrissey and Carol L. Osborne, *Amelia, My Courageous Sister: Biography of Amelia Earhart* (Santa Clara, Calif.: Osborne Publisher, 1987), p. 44.

3. Ibid.

4. Susan Butler, *East to the Dawn* (Reading, Mass.: Addison-Wesley, 1997), p. 77.

5. Jean L. Backus, *Letters from Amelia 1901–1937* (Boston: Beacon Press, 1982), p. 29.

6. Butler, p. 78.

7. Ibid., p. 79.

8. Earhart, p. 19.

9. Ibid., p. 20.

10. Amelia Earhart, *20 Hrs., 40 Min.* (New York: G. P. Putnam's Sons, 1928), p. 37.

11. Earhart, p. 20.

12. Earhart, *Last Flight* (New York: Crown Trade Paperbacks, 1968), p. 3.

13. Mary S. Lovell, *The Sound of Wings: The Life of Amelia Earhart* (New York: St. Martin's Press, 1968), p. 30.

14. Earhart, *The Fun of It*, p. 25.

15. Neta Snook Southern, *I Taught Amelia to Fly* (New York: Vantage Press, 1974), p. 1.

16. Lovell, p. 40.

17. Earhart, *20 Hrs., 40 Min.*, p. 54.

18. Morrissey and Osborne, p. 63.

19. Earhart, *The Fun of It*, p. 26.

20. Ibid., p. 27.

21. Lovell, p. 44.

22. Ibid.

23. Earhart, *The Fun of It*, p. 28.

Chapter 6. Social Work and Aviation

1. Amelia Earhart, *The Fun of It* (Chicago, Ill.: Academy Chicago Publishers, 1932), p. 57.

2. Mary S. Lovell, *The Sound of Wings: The Life of Amelia Earhart* (New York: St. Martin's Press, 1968), p. 48.

3. Ibid., p. 49.

4. Ibid., p. 50.

5. Susan Butler, *East to the Dawn* (Reading, Mass.: Addison-Wesley, 1997), p. 133.

6. Ibid., p. 136.

7. Ibid., p. 138.

8. Ibid., p. 153.

9. Hilton H. Railey, "Preface to Greatness, This World," *San Francisco Chronicle*, vol. 2, no. 21, September 11, 1938.

10. Earhart, p. 60.

11. Lovell, p. 92.

12. Donald M. Goldstein and Katherine V. Dillon, *Amelia: A Life of the Aviation Legend* (Washington, D.C.: Brassey's, 1999), p. 41.

13. Doris L. Rich, *Amelia Earhart: A Biography* (Washington, D.C.: Smithsonian Institution Press, 1989), p. 49.

14. Ibid.

15. Goldstein and Dillon, p. 43.

16. Earhart, p. 74.

17. Ibid., p. 76.

18. Amelia Earhart, *20 Hrs., 40 Min.* (New York: G. P. Putnam's Sons, 1928), p. 176.

Chapter 7. Celebrity

1. Donald M. Goldstein and Katherine V. Dillon, *Amelia: A Life of the Aviation Legend* (Washington, D.C.: Brassey's, 1999), p. 60.

2. Jean L. Backus, *Letters from Amelia 1901–1937* (Boston: Beacon Press, 1982), p. 75.

3. Mary S. Lovell, *The Sound of Wings: The Life of Amelia Earhart* (New York: St. Martin's Press, 1968), p. 122.

4. Goldstein and Dillon, p. 41.

5. Lovell, p. 123.

6. Muriel Earhart Morrissey and Carol L. Osborne, *Amelia, My Courageous Sister: Biography of Amelia Earhart* (Santa Clara, Calif.: Osborne Publisher, 1987), p. 87.

7. Ibid., p. 88.

8. Goldstein and Dillon, p. 54.

9. Morrissey and Osborne, p. 88.

10. Backus, p. 76.

11. Goldstein and Dillon, p. 61.

12. Lovell, p. 135.

13. Backus, p. 80.

14. Ibid.

15. Doris L. Rich, *Amelia Earhart: A Biography* (Washington, D.C.: Smithsonian Institution Press, 1989), p. 76.

16. Morrissey and Osborne, p. 101.

17. Lovell, p. 137.

18. Morrissey and Osborne, p. 101.

19. Ibid., p. 106.

Chapter 8. Queen of the Air

1. Doris L. Rich, *Amelia Earhart a Biography* (Washington, D.C.: Smithsonian Institution Press, 1989), p. 140.

2. Susan Butler, *East to the Dawn* (Reading, Mass.: Addison-Wesley, 1997), p. 230.

3. Ibid., p. 233.

4. Muriel Earhart Morrissey and Carol L. Osborne, *Amelia, My Courageous Sister: Biography of Amelia Earhart* (Santa Clara, Calif.: Osborne Publisher, 1987), p. 113.

5. Ibid.

6. Mary S. Lovell, *The Sound of Wings: The Life of Amelia Earhart* (New York: St. Martin's Press, 1968), p. 161.

7. Ibid., p. 154.

8. George Putnam, *Soaring Wings* (New York: Harcourt, Brace, & Co., 1939), p. 76.

9. Doris L. Rich, *Amelia Earhart: A Biography* (Washington, D.C.: Smithsonian Institution Press, 1989), p. 129.

10. Ibid.

11. Ibid.

12. Donald M. Goldstein and Katherine V. Dillon, *Amelia: A Life of the Aviation Legend* (Washington, D.C.: Brassey's, 1999), p. 122.

13. Rich, p. 136.

14. Goldstein and Dillon, p. 104.

15. Ibid., p. 105.

16. Susan Ware, *Still Missing: Amelia Earhart and the Search for Modern Feminism* (New York: W. W. Norton & Company, 1993), p. 99.

17. Ware, p. 101.

Chapter 9. Flights and More Flights

1. Susan Ware, *Still Missing: Amelia Earhart and the Search for Modern Feminism* (New York: W. W. Norton & Company, 1993), p. 61.

2. Donald M. Goldstein and Katherine V. Dillon, *Amelia: A Life of the Aviation Legend* (Washington, D.C.: Brassey's, 1999), p. 122.

3. Ibid., p. 123.

4. Muriel Earhart Morrissey and Carol L. Osborne, *Amelia, My Courageous Sister: Biography of Amelia Earhart* (Santa Clara, Calif.: Osborne Publisher, 1987), p. 150.

5. Goldstein and Dillon, p. 127.

6. Ibid.

7. Ibid., p. 129.

8. Amelia Earhart, "My Flight From Hawaii," *National Geographic*, May 1935, p. 592.

9. Ibid., p. 593.

10. Ibid., p. 594.

11. Amelia Earhart, *Last Flight* (New York: Crown Trade Paperbacks, 1968), p. 13.

12. Earhart, "My Flight From Hawaii," p. 594.

13. Ibid., p. 595.

14. Doris L. Rich, *Amelia Earhart a Biography* (Washington, D.C.: Smithsonian Institution Press, 1989), p. 201.

15. Goldstein and Dillon, p. 137.

16. Ibid.

17. Earhart, *Last Flight*, p. 23.

18. Ibid.

19. Ware, p. 209.

20. Earhart, *Last Flight*, p. 27.

21. Ware, p. 211.

22. George Putnam, *Soaring Wings* (New York: Harcourt, Brace, & Co., 1939), p. 272.

Chapter 10. Around the World

1. Muriel Earhart Morrissey and Carol L. Osborne, *Amelia, My Courageous Sister: Biography of Amelia Earhart* (Santa Clara, Calif.: Osborne Publisher, 1987), p. 193.

2. Amelia Earhart, *Last Flight* (New York: Crown Trade Paperbacks, 1968), p. 27.

3. Susan Butler, *East to the Dawn* (Reading, Mass.: Addison-Wesley, 1997), p. 346.

4. Earhart, p. 29.

5. Butler, p. 377.

6. Jean L. Backus, *Letters from Amelia 1901–1937* (Boston: Beacon Press, 1982), p. 212.

7. Ibid., p. 217.

8. Butler, p. 394.

9. Donald M. Goldstein and Katherine V. Dillon, *Amelia: A Life of the Aviation Legend* (Washington, D.C.: Brassey's, 1999), p. 206.

10. Backus, p. 229.

11. Butler, p. 396.

12. Ibid.

13. Earhart, p. 133.

14. Morrissey and Osborne, p. 232.

15. Elgen M. Long and Marie K. Long, *Amelia Earhart: The Mystery Solved* (New York: Simon and Schuster, 1999), p. 30.

Chapter 11. Epilogue

1. Muriel Earhart Morrissey and Carol L. Osborne, *Amelia, My Courageous Sister: Biography of Amelia Earhart* (Santa Clara, Calif.: Osborne Publisher, 1987), p. 74.

2. Donald M. Goldstein and Katherine V. Dillon, *Amelia: A Life of the Aviation Legend* (Washington, D.C.: Brassey's, 1999), p. 275.

3. Mary S. Lovell, *The Sound of Wings: The Life of Amelia Earhart* (New York: St. Martin's Press, 1968), pp. 359–360.

4. Joanne Cavanaugh Simpson, "Looking for Amelia," *Johns Hopkins Magazine*, June 2002, <http://www.jhu.edu/~jhumag/0602web/amelia.html> (August 28, 2002).

Glossary

air speed indicator—A flight instrument that shows air speed.

audit—To attend (a class or course) as a listener without receiving academic credit.

control panel—A panel containing the instruments, switches, gauges, or other devices for the management and control of an airplane.

corroded—Eaten away, due to a chemical reaction.

course—The direction taken by an aircraft, often expressed in degrees.

debutante—A young woman making her first formal appearance in society.

extracurricular—Outside the regular course of study; such as sports, dramatics, or clubs.

fee for service—A fee for professional services that is paid after the service has been provided.

patent—A government grant that gives a person sole rights to make, use, or sell a new invention for a certain number of years.

piecemeal—Done piece by piece or a little at a time.

pontoons—One or two hollow metal containers fastened to the bottom of an airplane so that it can land on water and float.

stunt flying—Performing dangerous or difficult feats in an airplane to gain attention or entertain.

taxiing—An airplane's slow movement on the ground before gathering speed to take off or after landing.

ticker tape—Cellophane or paper tape on which a telegraphic instrument ticker prints stock-market reports or news.

FURTHER READING AND INTERNET ADDRESSES

Books

Adler, David. *A Picture Book of Amelia Earhart*. New York: Holiday House, 1998.

Goldstein, Donald M., and Katherine V. Dillon. *Amelia: A Life of the Aviation Legend*. Washington, D.C.: Brassey's, 1997.

Kent, Zachary. *Charles Lindbergh and the* Spirit of St. Louis *in American History*. Berkeley Heights, N.J.: Enslow Publishers, Inc., 2001.

Parr, Jan. *Amelia Earhart: First Lady of Flight*. Danbury, Conn.: Franklin Watts, 1997.

Szabo, Corrine. *Sky Pioneer: A Photobiography of Amelia Earhart*. Washington, D.C.: National Geographic Society, 1997.

Ware, Susan. *Still Missing: Amelia Earhart and the Search for Modern Feminism*. New York: W. W. Norton, 1993.

Internet Addresses

Amelia Earhart Birthplace Museum. n.d. <http://www.ameliaearhartmuseum.org/>.

The Ninety-Nines. *The Ninety-Nines, Inc., International Organization of Women Pilots*. n.d. <http://www.ninety-nines.org/>.

Smithsonian, National Air and Space Museum, Aeronautics Division. *Women in Aviation and Space History: Amelia Earhart*. n.d. <http://www.nasm.si.edu/nasm/aero/women_aviators/amelia_earhart>.

INDEX